PASSING THE BACKGROUND

A Police Background Investigator's Complete Guide

for Peace Officer Applicants

How the Hiring Process Really Works, Stage by Stage — and How to Get Through It Honestly

A Veteran Peace Officer & Background Investigator

This guide offers general educational information based on common practices across U.S. law enforcement agencies. It does not represent the policy of any specific agency. Every department's process, forms, platforms, and disqualifiers differ — always follow the instructions your agency's recruiting and background unit gives you.

2026 Expanded Edition | Nationally oriented, with examples from official state POST/licensing systems and major testing providers. Agency and state requirements always control.
Published by BKD Digital Media

COPYRIGHT & PUBLICATION NOTICE

First expanded edition, 2026.

This publication is an independent educational resource. It is not sponsored, endorsed, approved, or issued by any law-enforcement agency, POST or licensing body, testing provider, background-investigation platform, psychologist, physician, polygraph examiner, or other third party mentioned in the text. Agency instructions, state law, and current official standards control.

Third-party names and marks - including POST agency names, National Testing Network/NTN, FrontLine, Guardian Alliance, eSOPH, and other identified products or organizations - are used only for identification, commentary, and factual reference. All trademarks, service marks, logos, copyrighted test materials, software, forms, screenshots, and other proprietary content remain the property of their respective owners.

Source-use policy for this edition: outside materials were used to verify facts, terminology, and current public standards. This book does not reproduce proprietary test questions, answer keys, vendor screenshots, third-party logos, or proprietary platform forms. Explanations, applicant guidance, examples, checklists, and worksheets are presented in original language, except for short names and labels necessary to identify official standards or services.

Research and source attribution: This publication combines the author's professional observations with research from publicly available government, regulatory, testing, and professional sources. The author brings more than 30 years of state law-enforcement experience: 30 years as a sworn officer and Sergeant, followed after retirement by one year conducting peace-officer backgrounds for contract agencies through a private company, one year conducting peace-officer and dispatcher backgrounds as a retired annuitant, and one year of current work conducting peace-officer and sworn-selection backgrounds for a state law-enforcement agency. That experience includes 15 years conducting background investigations, 10 years as a CVSA examiner, four years as a recruiter, and relevant field and instructor assignments. No current or former agency or employer is identified. Where an outside authority materially informs a section, that authority is identified in a research/source note and/or Appendix A.

Legal and professional disclaimer: this guide provides general educational information, not legal, medical, psychological, employment, or agency-specific advice. Requirements and disqualifiers differ by jurisdiction and agency and may change after publication. Applicants should follow the instructions of the agency to which they are applying and consult an appropriate licensed professional when individualized advice is needed.

Before You Put on the Badge

If you are reading this book, there is a good chance you have already pictured yourself wearing the uniform. Maybe this has been your goal since childhood. Maybe you are leaving the military, changing careers, finishing school, or looking for work that carries real purpose. Whatever brings you here, I want to help you navigate the hiring process. Before we talk about tests and forms, though, I want you to understand the profession you are working so hard to enter.

I spent 30 years as a sworn state law-enforcement officer and Sergeant. Since retiring, I have continued conducting peace-officer and other public-safety background investigations in private-contract, retired-annuitant, and state sworn-selection settings. Across my career, I have spent 15 years conducting backgrounds, 10 years as a CVSA examiner, and four years as a recruiter. I have also served in field and instructor assignments. I am telling you that so you know the perspective behind these pages - not so you will treat my experience as a substitute for your agency's current rules.

This profession did not begin with patrol cars, radios, body-worn cameras, or computerized records. Early American communities relied on sheriffs, constables, and night watches. Boston's official history traces its watch to 1631 and its transition to a unified police department in 1854. During the nineteenth century, growing cities developed permanent municipal police organizations. That history also includes discriminatory laws, unequal enforcement, corruption, and other failures that modern policing must acknowledge rather than erase. The point of this brief history is not to give you a textbook chapter. It is to remind you that policing has always changed with the society it serves.

The badge has changed. The uniform has changed. The equipment, law, training, and public expectations have changed. The responsibility has not.

Modern officers work in an environment earlier generations could not have imagined. A call may be recorded by dispatch, a body-worn camera, nearby security systems, and several phones. A decision made in seconds can later be replayed frame by frame. Policies are more detailed. Records are easier to retrieve. Courts, oversight bodies, supervisors, journalists, community members, and the public may all review what happened. Accountability is not an obstacle to professional policing; it is part of the authority society has entrusted to you.

Public perception is complicated

You are entering the profession at a time when public confidence is neither uniform nor guaranteed. Gallup's long-running survey reported that 45 percent of U.S. adults had a great deal or quite a lot of confidence in the police in 2026, compared with 64 percent at the high point shown in 2004. Those numbers do not tell us what every community or every person believes, but they do tell you that trust cannot be assumed.

When an officer commits serious misconduct, the incident deserves investigation, accountability, and public scrutiny. A badge does not excuse dishonesty, criminal behavior, unnecessary force, or abuse of authority. Officers who betray the public trust damage more than their own careers; they create consequences for colleagues and communities that have nothing to do with their conduct.

At the same time, highly unusual events naturally receive far more attention than ordinary professional work. The Bureau of Justice Statistics estimated that 49.2 million U.S. residents age 16 or older had at least one police contact in 2022. Most routine contacts will never become national news: the collision report handled carefully, the impaired driver stopped before a crash, the frightened victim treated with patience, the missing person found, or the traffic stop completed professionally. That does not make misconduct reporting unfair or dishonest. It means that memorable incidents can shape how people see the uniform you are about to wear.

You inherit some of the trust earned by officers who came before you, and you also inherit some of the distrust created by officers who failed it. Your conduct either adds to that trust or takes away from it.

Your routine contact may change someone else's life

During a law-enforcement career, you may have thousands of contacts with people. Eventually, some of them can start to feel routine. Do not let them.

That traffic stop may be your eighth contact of the shift. For the person you stopped, it may be the first time they have ever spoken with a police officer. The arrest you are processing may be one of hundreds in your career. For the person in handcuffs and for that person's family, it may be an event remembered for the rest of their lives. Even a citation can affect finances, a driving record, employment, or family responsibilities.

You can be firm without being disrespectful. You can make an arrest without humiliating someone. You can issue a citation and still explain what you are doing. You can control a dangerous situation while using restraint and treating people with dignity. Sometimes a person will resent you regardless of how professionally you act. Be professional anyway. That is the job.

Why the career is still worth it

I would not have stayed in this profession for three decades if I did not believe the work could matter. Law enforcement will put you beside people during fear, grief, conflict, and danger. You may prevent harm that no one else ever knows was about to happen. You may bring order to a moment that feels impossible to everyone involved. You may become the calm voice a person remembers years later. Those rewards are real, but they come with fatigue, criticism, missed holidays, imperfect outcomes, and decisions that carry weight.

So before you put on the badge, ask yourself a harder question than whether you can pass the hiring process: Are you willing to accept the responsibility that comes after it? If your answer is yes, I will walk you through what is coming, why each stage matters, where applicants create avoidable problems, and how to prepare without pretending to be someone you are not.

Research note: Historical details are drawn from the Boston Police Department's official history. Police-contact estimates are from the U.S. Bureau of Justice Statistics, Contacts Between Police and the Public, 2022 (published 2024). Confidence figures are from Gallup's Confidence in Institutions historical series, updated in 2026. These sourced facts are distinct from the author's professional observations.

Contents

Use this contents list to locate each chapter and major section in the paperback edition.

Chapter 1: How the Hiring Process Really Works

If you've started researching how to become a police officer, you've probably noticed the process feels long, opaque, and a little intimidating. I've sat on the other side of that process for years — reading files, making calls, sitting across the table from candidates and their neighbors, and deciding whether to recommend someone move forward. This guide pulls back the curtain. Not to help you cheat the process, but to help you understand it well enough that you can walk through it with confidence and give your honest best at every stage.

The typical sequence

Most agencies follow a version of the same sequence, though the order, the names of each stage, and exactly which stages exist vary by department, state, and civil service rules:

1. Application and minimum qualifications screening (age, citizenship, education, driving record, criminal history thresholds)
2. Physical abilities test (PAT/PFT)
3. Written examination
4. Oral board interview (sometimes more than one round)
5. Conditional offer of employment
6. Background investigation
7. Polygraph or voice stress examination (where permitted by state law)
8. Psychological evaluation
9. Medical examination, including drug screening
10. Final review by the chief, sheriff, hiring board, or civil service commission
11. Academy

Some agencies run these in parallel to save time (for example, scheduling your medical and psych appointments during the background investigation window); others run them strictly in sequence and won't schedule your polygraph until your background file is substantially complete. Ask your recruiter for your agency's specific order and expected timeline — most processes take anywhere from three to nine months start to finish, sometimes longer for agencies with high applicant volume or civil service list systems.

The shift in what's being measured

Here's the thing most applicants don't fully appreciate: everything after the conditional offer is really one long integrity check. The written test and physical test measure whether you can do the job. Everything from the background investigation forward measures whether you can be trusted with a badge, a gun, a patrol car, and access to other people's worst days, most private information, and most vulnerable moments. That shift in focus — from capability to character — is the single most important thing to understand as you prepare.

> *— Veteran background investigator with 15 years of experience*

Why the process feels redundant

Applicants often ask why they have to answer the same questions about drug use, finances, and personal conduct on the PHS, again in the background interview, again to the polygrapher, and again to the psychologist. It's not bureaucratic redundancy — it's a deliberate design. Each stage is a different way of checking whether your story holds together. Investigators, polygraphers, and psychologists compare notes. A minor inconsistency between what you told your background investigator and what you told the psychologist is often more damaging than the underlying fact you were inconsistent about.

Understanding disqualifiers: absolute vs. discretionary

Most agencies operate with two tiers of disqualifying factors, though the specific list is set by state POST (Peace Officer Standards and Training) regulations and local policy:

Typically Absolute (agency and state dependent)	Typically Discretionary / Totality-of-Circumstances
Certain felony convictions	Older misdemeanor convictions
Domestic violence convictions (federal firearms prohibition)	Isolated financial trouble, resolved or being managed
Dishonorable military discharge	Occasional past recreational drug use outside the lookback window
Failing to meet citizenship/age/education minimums	A single at-fault traffic collision or moving violation pattern
Falsification discovered during the process itself	Youthful, non-violent mistakes with clear growth since

The right column is where most applicants actually live, and where honest disclosure combined with context and growth matters enormously. The left column is largely out of your control by the time you apply — the right column is where your preparation and honesty make the real difference.

Phase 0: Before You Apply

A strong application starts before the application opens. Read the job announcement line by line, confirm minimum qualifications, disqualifiers, testing deadlines, score-transfer rules, fee-waiver rules, residency or driver-license requirements, tattoo/grooming policies, and document requirements. Do not assume one agency's rules transfer to another. Official POST/licensing standards are often minimums; local departments may set higher standards.

Pre-application check	What to verify
Minimum qualifications	Age, education, work authorization/citizenship rules where applicable, driver-license status, criminal-history restrictions and state certification requirements.
Testing path	Which written test is accepted, whether prior scores transfer, PAT format, oral board format, and whether testing is remote or in person.
Documentation	Transcripts, DD-214/service documents if applicable, driver record, certifications, legal dispositions, employment dates and contact information.
Disqualifiers	Read the agency's published automatic and discretionary criteria. If something is unclear, ask recruiting—not social media.
Communication	Use a stable email account, professional voicemail, and calendar reminders. Check spam/junk folders daily while active in a process.

Application accuracy audit

Before submitting, compare the application against your resume, prior applications, PHS drafts, school dates, employment dates, addresses, citations, military history, and any prior public-safety applications. A typo is different from deception, but repeated unexplained inconsistencies can create avoidable work and credibility questions later.

Important distinction
A conditional offer is not a guaranteed appointment. In many jurisdictions, medical and psychological examinations occur only after a conditional offer because federal disability law limits pre-offer medical inquiries and examinations. Agencies may still administer job-related physical ability tests before an offer.

From the Recruiter's Desk

During four years in recruiting, I learned that applicants often think the hiring process begins when they click Submit. It begins earlier - with the way you research the agency, read the announcement, communicate with recruiters, and decide whether this particular department and community fit you.

Talk to a recruiter for information, not reassurance. Ask what test is used, whether an official study guide exists, what the physical events and standards are, which documents take time to obtain, and what changes must be reported after application. A recruiter can explain the process; a recruiter cannot promise that you will be selected or excuse you from a published requirement.

Research more than pay and uniforms. Look at jurisdiction, call volume, staffing, training, specialty opportunities, schedule expectations, community priorities, labor agreements where public, and recent public reports. If you apply to several agencies, keep a separate file for each. Copying an answer from one application into another without reading the new question is one of the easiest ways to create an inconsistency.

Chapter 2: The Physical Ability Test and Written Examination

The Physical Abilities Test

Whether your agency uses a PAT circuit (obstacle course, dummy drag, trigger pull, stair climb) or a fitness-standard test (push-ups, sit-ups, timed run, sometimes a bench press or vertical jump), the test is pass/fail for a reason: it reflects a real minimum standard tied to the physical demands of the job. Train specifically for the test format your agency uses, not just general fitness.

Common test components

Component	What it measures	How to train it
1.5-mile run or 300m sprint	Cardiovascular endurance / anaerobic capacity	Interval training 2–3x/week; one longer steady-state run weekly
Push-ups / sit-ups (timed)	Muscular endurance	High-rep sets 3–4x/week; focus on strict form, not just count
Dummy drag (typically 165 lb.)	Functional strength, grip, technique	Practice the actual movement — technique matters as much as raw strength
6-foot wall / obstacle course	Agility, explosive power, coordination	Practice on an actual wall or similar obstacle if you can access one
Trigger pull (simulated)	Finger/hand strength and endurance	Grip trainers and repeated trigger-pull practice with the required weight

Sample 6-week training approach

- Weeks 1–2: Build a base — 3 cardio sessions, 2 full-body strength sessions, technique work on any circuit-specific movements.
- Weeks 3–4: Add intensity — interval sprints, timed practice runs of the actual PAT circuit if available.
- Weeks 5–6: Taper and sharpen — reduce volume slightly, keep intensity, rehearse the exact test sequence once or twice, prioritize sleep.
- Test week: Hydrate well, eat a normal familiar meal beforehand, and avoid trying anything new (new shoes, new supplements, a new pre-workout) on test day.

> *Applicants fail the PAT far more often from poor pacing and unfamiliarity with the specific obstacles than from lack of fitness. Practice the actual*

> *test, not just 'fitness' in the abstract.*

Physical Ability Test: train the test, not the myth

PATs vary dramatically. Some use runs, push-ups and sit-ups; others use obstacle courses, wall climbs, dummy drags, stairs, trigger-pull simulations, or job-task circuits. Get the agency's current event list, sequence, scoring rules and required form. A standard that appears in another department's video may be irrelevant to your test.

PAT preparation principles

Build aerobic capacity, short-burst recovery, lower-body power, pulling/grip strength and movement efficiency. Rehearse transitions between events because cumulative fatigue—not a single event—often determines performance. If you have a medical concern, seek appropriate medical guidance; do not use this guide as medical clearance.

ADA note
Federal guidance distinguishes job-related physical agility/fitness tests from medical examinations. An agency may administer a task/fitness test pre-offer, while medical examinations are generally restricted until after a conditional offer.

From the Field: Physical readiness

The physical test is not the job, and passing it does not make you ready for every physical demand of police work. From field and instructor experience, I can tell you that agencies also need people who can listen under stress, move safely, recover, and follow the approved method. Train progressively for the published events, practice safe technique, and seek medical guidance if you have health concerns. Do not arrive injured because you tried to become fit in one frantic week.

The Written Exam

Entry-level written testing is not standardized nationwide. An agency may use a state-developed examination, a commercial testing provider, a civil-service examination, or a locally validated instrument. California POST's PELLETB and National Testing Network's FrontLine National are examples of different testing approaches. Before studying, identify the exact examination your agency accepts and use that provider's current official candidate information.

What's typically tested

- Reading comprehension: short passages followed by fact-based questions
- Grammar, spelling, and report-writing mechanics

- Basic arithmetic and word problems (time/distance, percentages, basic statistics)
- Memory and observation: study a photo or narrative, then answer questions from memory later in the test
- Situational judgment: multiple-choice scenarios asking how you would respond to a hypothetical incident

How to prepare

- Get the study guide matched to the specific test your agency uses — they are not interchangeable, and generic 'police exam' books sometimes cover the wrong format.
- Take at least two full-length timed practice tests under real conditions (no phone, no notes, timed) so pacing isn't a surprise.
- Review basic grammar and punctuation rules — apostrophes, subject-verb agreement, and run-on sentences are the most commonly missed items.
- For memory/observation sections, practice the specific technique of scanning a photo systematically (foreground to background, left to right) rather than trying to memorize everything at once.
- For situational-judgment questions, choose the answer that reflects patience, de-escalation, and following policy — not the most aggressive or fastest-resolution option.

From the Recruiter's Desk: Written testing

I want you to prepare for the test the agency actually uses, not for a generic police exam you found online. Obtain the official candidate guide when one exists. Learn the sections, timing, permitted materials, identification rules, retest policy, and whether scores may transfer. Practice reading accurately under time pressure, but do not chase stolen questions or supposed answer keys.

Your score is only part of what I notice. Following check-in instructions, arriving early, bringing the required identification, and handling frustration professionally are small demonstrations of the habits the job will require.

Know the Exact Written Test You Are Taking

Research note: California POST PELLETB FAQs and National Testing Network FrontLine National, reviewed August 2026.

There is no single national 'police written test.' Current official materials illustrate how formats differ. California POST's PELLETB evaluates language and reading-related skills and no longer includes the former CLOZE subtest. National Testing Network describes FrontLine National as combining a video-based judgment/human-relations portion with reading and report-writing components. The hiring agency determines which test it accepts and may establish its own score, ranking, or validity requirements.

Test area	Practice that transfers well

Reading	Read policy-like passages; identify facts, sequence, exceptions, and the best supported conclusion.
Writing mechanics	Practice concise sentences, grammar, punctuation, spelling, and removing ambiguity.
Report writing	Describe only observable facts, use chronological order, separate what you saw from what someone told you, and avoid unsupported conclusions.
Situational judgment	Choose lawful, proportionate, professional responses that prioritize safety, communication, teamwork and policy compliance.
Timed performance	Practice under the same time limits and interface/format used by the provider whenever possible.

A 14-day written-test plan

Days 1–2: identify the exact test and obtain the official candidate guide. Days 3–6: diagnose weaknesses with practice questions. Days 7–10: drill the weakest two areas. Days 11–12: complete timed simulations. Day 13: light review only. Day 14/test day: arrive rested, follow identification and prohibited-item rules, and pace yourself.

Chapter 3: The Oral Board Interview

The oral board is usually a panel of two to five people — often a mix of patrol officers, detectives, command staff, a human resources representative, and sometimes a community member. They are scoring you against a written rubric, not having a casual conversation, even when it feels conversational. Most panels score each answer on a numeric scale and total the scores at the end, so a strong opening answer doesn't make up for a weak one later.

From the Recruiter's Desk: The oral board

When I coached applicants as a recruiter, I did not want a memorized speech. I wanted a person who had researched the agency, could organize an answer, listened to the full question, and gave specific examples. Build a bank of true experiences involving conflict, accountability, teamwork, ethical pressure, service, failure, and learning. Know the facts well enough to speak naturally; do not script every sentence.

If you receive a scenario, explain your priorities before racing to a tactical answer: protect life, obtain needed information, request resources, act within law and policy, communicate, and reassess. The board understands that an entry-level applicant has not yet been trained as an officer. It is evaluating judgment and communication, not whether you can imitate a veteran officer.

What panels are actually scoring

- Communication: Can you explain yourself clearly, in complete thoughts, under mild pressure and time constraints?
- Judgment: Do your answers to hypothetical scenarios show restraint, de-escalation, and reasoning — or do they jump straight to force or extreme outcomes?
- Self-awareness: Can you talk honestly about a mistake or weakness without becoming defensive or over-explaining?
- Motivation: Do you have a genuine, specific reason for wanting this job at this agency, or a generic answer that could apply anywhere?
- Composure: How do you handle a follow-up question designed to probe or gently push back on your first answer?

Common question categories

Category	Example prompt	What a strong answer shows

Motivation	Why this department, and why now?	Specific research about the agency and a coherent personal timeline
Ethics/integrity	Describe a time you saw someone break a rule. What did you do?	Willingness to act, without grandstanding
Scenario/judgment	A friend asks you to fix a ticket once you're an officer. What do you say?	Clear, immediate boundary without hesitation
Self-reflection	What's a mistake you've made and what did you learn?	A real example, ownership, and a concrete lesson
Stress/conflict	Tell us about a disagreement with a supervisor or coworker.	Calm description, respect for the other party, resolution

Preparation tips

- Use a simple structure for behavioral questions: describe the Situation, the Task, the Action you took, and the Result (the STAR method).
- Prepare four or five real examples from work, school, military, or volunteer experience that show integrity, teamwork, and conflict resolution — you can usually adapt the same story to several different questions.
- Research the specific department: its size, community demographics, any specialized units, recent initiatives, so your 'why this agency' answer isn't generic.
- Practice out loud in a mock panel with friends or a mentor, so the first time you say your answers isn't in the actual interview.
- Dress and arrive as if this were the actual job — panels do factor in professionalism and punctuality, even informally.

> *Panels remember the candidate who said 'I made a mistake and here's what I learned' far more favorably than the one who insisted they'd never done anything wrong in their life.*

How to Prepare for a Structured Oral Board

Research note: California POST Interviewing Peace Officer Candidates and current selection standards.

Structured oral boards commonly use the same or comparable questions for candidates and evaluate answers against predetermined job-related factors. As one public example, California POST identifies six interview areas: experience, problem-solving, communication, interest/motivation, interpersonal skills, and community involvement/awareness. The applicant-facing explanations in the table below are this guide's own interpretation of those short competency labels; other jurisdictions may organize interview criteria differently.

Competency	What your answer should demonstrate
Experience	Relevant learning from work, school, military, volunteer or life experience—without overstating your role.
Problem-solving	You gather facts, identify priorities, consider options, explain tradeoffs and choose a defensible action.
Communication	Clear structure, direct answers, appropriate detail, professional language and active listening.
Interest / motivation	A specific, researched reason for public service and for this agency—not prestige, authority or excitement alone.
Interpersonal skills	Respect, teamwork, conflict management, empathy, boundaries and accountability.
Community awareness	Understanding of the community, service expectations, diversity of viewpoints and the agency's current priorities.

Build a story bank, not a script

Prepare 6–8 true stories that cover integrity, conflict, teamwork, failure, learning, stress, initiative, customer/community service, difficult feedback and a decision made with incomplete information. Use STAR as an organizing tool, but answer naturally. Panels can usually tell when an applicant is forcing a memorized speech onto a question.

For scenario questions

State your immediate priority, explain what facts you would need, identify safety/legal/policy considerations, describe communication and de-escalation where appropriate, and explain when you would seek a supervisor or additional resources. Do not invent department-specific policy you have not been taught.

Avoid the "perfect candidate" trap
A strong interview answer can acknowledge uncertainty, a past mistake, or a need to consult policy. Overconfident absolutes—especially about use of force, discipline, ethics or legal authority—can make judgment look weaker, not stronger.

Chapter 4: Inside the Background Investigation

This is where I've spent most of my career, so let me be direct and thorough about what actually happens and what actually matters.

From the Background Investigator's Desk

This is the part of the process where I want you to stop managing an image and start building an accurate record. During 15 years of background work, I have seen applicants survive difficult history when they disclosed it clearly, accepted responsibility, and showed change. I have also seen ordinary issues become serious because an applicant minimized, omitted, or changed the story after records and interviews filled in the gaps. I am not promising that honesty makes every fact acceptable. I am telling you that dishonesty creates a separate suitability problem.

What we are really evaluating

A background investigation is not a search for a perfect person — perfect people don't exist, and every experienced investigator knows it. We are evaluating a narrower set of questions:

- Is this person honest, including about their own flaws?
- Do they have a pattern of poor judgment, or isolated incidents consistent with normal growth?
- Can they be trusted with authority, firearms, confidential information, and vulnerable people?
- How does this person behave when no one with power over them is watching — with peers, strangers, and people who can't help or hurt their career?
- Is there anything in their history that would embarrass the department, create civil liability, or be used to impeach their credibility in court (a Brady/Giglio issue)?

Almost nothing in a candidate's past is automatically disqualifying on its own. Nearly everything becomes disqualifying when it's combined with dishonesty about it during the process.

The investigator's toolkit

A typical background investigation draws on several sources, cross-checked against each other:

- Your Personal History Statement (PHS) and any supplemental questionnaires

- Certified records: criminal history, driving record, credit report, court records, military records
- Employment verification calls to every listed employer, plus any employers we find that you didn't list
- Education verification with schools and, where relevant, licensing boards
- A field interview with you, often after the file review, to resolve open questions face to face
- Interviews with the references you provide
- Interviews with collateral contacts you did not select — neighbors, former roommates, and others (see Chapter 5)
- A review of publicly available social media and online presence
- In some agencies, a home visit or neighborhood canvass

Paper packet vs. online PHS platforms (Guardian, eSOPH, and similar systems)

Historically, the PHS was a thick paper packet you filled out by hand or typewriter and mailed or hand-delivered to the background unit. Many agencies still do this, especially smaller departments with limited technology budgets. But a growing number of agencies — and many larger, better-funded ones — have moved to online background investigation platforms, most commonly Guardian Alliance Technologies or eSOPH, with a handful of agencies using other proprietary systems. Which platform (or paper form) your agency uses generally comes down to agency size and budget, not the thoroughness of the investigation itself; a paper packet and an online profile are asking for the same information.

These platforms typically have you build a profile and enter your history directly into a web portal rather than a paper form. Several features are worth understanding before you start:

- The system usually generates automated reference and employment-verification requests — often by email — the moment you enter a contact's information and submit that section.
- Some systems send your listed references a self-service questionnaire link directly, meaning the reference completes part of the process without ever speaking to the investigator by phone first.
- Entries are frequently locked or hard to revise once submitted, so accuracy on first entry matters even more than it does with a paper form you can proofread and correct before mailing.
- Because these systems often work off whatever contact information you type in, a wrong digit in a phone number or a mistyped email address doesn't just slow things down — it can cause an entire reference or employer verification to silently fail and never reach the person at all.

Why current phone numbers and valid email addresses both matter

Gather a current phone number AND a current, regularly checked email address for every single person you plan to list — not one or the other. Online systems increasingly rely on email to reach references and employers directly, and a bounced or abandoned email address can stall your background before an investigator ever knows there's a problem.

It's easy to assume a phone number is enough, especially for people you talk to often. But people change jobs and lose access to old work email addresses; personal email addresses get abandoned for years at a time; and some people simply don't check email that isn't tied to something they use daily. If an online system emails a reference request to an address that's dead, misspelled, or simply never checked, that reference can sit unanswered indefinitely, and neither you nor the reference may realize anything went wrong until your investigator asks why that section of your file is still empty.

- For every reference and collateral contact, confirm both a phone number and an email address directly with that person — don't rely on an old number or address you have saved from years ago.
- Ask each person to actually check that they can access the email account you're listing, and to keep an eye out for a message from the background unit or the online platform in the weeks after you submit.
- If someone primarily uses a work email, get a personal email as a backup — people lose access to work accounts when they change jobs, sometimes with no notice.
- Double-check every phone number and email address for typos before you submit — a single wrong character is functionally the same as leaving that reference off your list entirely.

Whose job it is to gather this information

It is not the background investigator's job to track down contact information for the people you list. It is your job, as the applicant, to gather accurate, current phone numbers and email addresses before you ever start your PHS or online

> **profile — and to confirm that information directly with each person.**

This point gets lost on some applicants, who treat the reference and employment sections of the PHS as a rough draft the investigator will clean up. That's backwards. An investigator's job is to verify what you've told them — not to locate people for you, chase down a current number when the one you provided is disconnected, or guess at an email address because you weren't sure of the spelling. When contact information is wrong or outdated, the most common result isn't extra effort on the investigator's part; it's a stalled or incomplete background file, which reflects on you, not on the process.

Think of this as conducting your own background investigation on yourself before you submit anything. Before you sit down to complete a paper PHS or an online profile:

- Make your list of every employer, address, and reference you'll need to include, going back as far as the form requires.
- Contact each person directly — don't rely on memory, an old group chat, or a contact saved years ago.
- Confirm their current phone number and current email address, and ask which one they check most reliably.
- Let them know an investigator or an automated system may reach out, and roughly when, so a message from an unfamiliar background-check platform doesn't get ignored as spam.
- Keep your own organized record of this information so it's consistent across a paper PHS, an online profile, and anything you tell your investigator in person.

Agencies using Guardian, eSOPH, or a similar platform are, in a sense, asking you to do a version of an investigator's job before they ever start theirs: assemble accurate, verifiable information about your own history and make sure the people who can speak to it are reachable. Applicants who treat that as their own responsibility — rather than something the background unit will sort out — consistently move through this stage faster and with fewer complications.

The Personal History Statement (PHS)

Your PHS (sometimes called a background packet or personal data questionnaire) is the single most important document in your file. Investigators cross-check it obsessively against records, references, and interviews. Treat it like a sworn statement, because in most agencies it functions as one, and knowingly falsifying it is itself a disqualifying offense independent of whatever you were trying to hide.

- Answer every question completely — an incomplete answer is treated the same as a false one.
- List every address, employer, and reference for the full period requested, even ones that are inconvenient or embarrassing to include.
- Disclose juvenile records, expunged or sealed records, and diversion program participation if the form asks for them — 'legally cleared' does not mean it cannot be asked about on a government employment form, and most PHS forms are explicit about this.
- If you're unsure whether something counts (a warning citation, a workplace write-up, a one-time experimental drug use in college), disclose it and let the investigator make the call. Investigators forgive disclosed problems far more easily than discovered ones.
- Keep a personal timeline and document trail as you fill this out — dates of employment, supervisor names, addresses, roommates — so your PHS, your interview answers, and your polygraph are all consistent.

Residences

Build a residence history for your entire lifetime, even if the agency's current form asks for a shorter lookback period. That preparation gives you a reliable master record if another agency later asks for more. On the official form, answer the exact period requested; do not omit an address that falls within that period and do not invent dates to force a perfect timeline.

- For every residence, record the complete street address, city, state, ZIP code, and the month and year you moved in and out.
- Identify the landlord, property manager, homeowner, or other person who can verify the residence, with a current phone number and email address when reasonably available.
- List every roommate or other adult who shared the residence during the period requested, including former partners when the form requires them, and keep current contact information when you can lawfully obtain it.
- Account for temporary housing, military quarters, dormitories, extended stays with relatives or friends, and periods without a conventional address whenever the agency asks for them.
- Check the sequence against school, employment, tax, lease, utility, and military records. Explain honest gaps or overlaps instead of guessing.

From the Background Investigator's Desk: Residence history is not busywork. It helps me verify chronology and identify landlords, neighbors, and former roommates who may have observed a different part of your life. A complete private lifetime worksheet keeps you prepared, but the agency's PHS and instructions always control what you submit.

Drug Use

Drug questions are where applicants sometimes try to summarize, soften, or combine events. Do not do that. Prepare a complete lifetime inventory of every illegal drug or narcotic you have used and every prescription medication you used illegally. Then answer each agency question exactly as written. If it asks about your entire lifetime, disclose every use. If it specifies a lookback period, answer that period completely and follow any instruction requiring older conduct to be reported.

For each specific substance, be ready to document:

- The name of the drug or medication, your age at each period of use, the approximate date of first use, and the date of last use.
- How it was ingested or administered and, as accurately as you can reconstruct it, how many times you used or tried that specific substance.
- Whether you purchased, manufactured, cultivated, carried, possessed, transported, furnished, gave away, held for another person, transported for sale, or sold the substance, with dates, frequency, circumstances, and outcome.
- Whether the conduct occurred while employed in public safety, while holding a position of trust or security clearance, while driving, at work, in the military, or in another circumstance specifically asked about by the form.
- Whether you associated with friends, acquaintances, housemates, or family members who illegally possessed or used drugs or narcotics, or illegally used prescription medication, when the form asks about those associations. Describe what you actually knew, when you knew it, your own involvement, and whether the association continued.

Do not estimate downward to make the history look better. If you cannot remember an exact count, make a good-faith reconstruction from dates, people, places, messages, calendars, or other lawful records, identify the answer as an estimate when the form permits, and explain the basis for it. Separate your own conduct from conduct you merely witnessed, but disclose both when the question requires it.

From the Background Investigator's Desk: Prior drug use is evaluated under the hiring agency's current law and policy, including the type of substance, recency, frequency, surrounding conduct, evidence of change, and candor. A disclosed issue can be evaluated. An omission that is contradicted by records, references, or your later interview creates a separate integrity problem.

Employment and education verification

We contact every employer you list, not just the ones you'd prefer we call, and we usually ask directly whether you are 'eligible for rehire.' We ask about attendance, punctuality, how you handled conflict with coworkers or supervisors, and any disciplinary history. Gaps in employment aren't a problem by themselves — unexplained or misrepresented gaps are. If you were terminated, disclose it and be ready to explain what happened and what you learned; we will call and ask the employer's version regardless.

Military

If you were required to register with the Selective Service System, verify your registration status and keep the confirmation information. Under current federal rules, almost all male U.S. citizens and male immigrants ages 18 through 25 must register, with limited exceptions. The agency's question, applicable law, and your individual circumstances control; if you are uncertain, use the official Selective Service status-verification process rather than guessing.

If you have served in the United States Armed Forces, National Guard, or Reserves, prepare a complete service history that includes:

- Branch or component, dates of service, duty status, units, duty stations, assignments, ranks, occupational specialties, deployments, and whether you are currently serving in a Reserve or National Guard component.
- The character and type of every discharge or separation, and a copy of each DD Form 214 or equivalent separation document that applies to your service.
- Any nonjudicial punishment (NJP), Article 15 or Captain's Mast proceeding, court-martial, administrative action, counseling, reprimand, reduction, adverse evaluation, investigation, or other discipline requested by the form.
- Any military property taken, retained, damaged, transferred, or used without permission; any security clearance that was denied, suspended, revoked, or restricted; and the facts and outcome of each event.
- Any combat service or deployment the form asks you to identify. State the facts without embellishment and distinguish an official combat designation from your personal description of an assignment.

Request your own Official Military Personnel File (OMPF) early enough to review it before submission. The National Archives explains that an OMPF can contain assignments, training, performance, awards, disciplinary actions, administrative remarks, and separation information, including the DD Form 214. Veterans may request records through the National Archives' eVetRecs process or with Standard Form 180, subject to record location and access rules. A hiring agency may use its own release or request process, so follow the investigator's instructions and do not send sensitive records through an unapproved channel.

From the Background Investigator's Desk: Military service can demonstrate responsibility, leadership, resilience, and teamwork, but it is still verified like every other part of the file. Give the investigator the full record, including accomplishments and adverse matters. Do not assume an NJP, discharge characterization, missing DD Form 214, or clearance issue will explain itself.

Financial history

We typically review a credit report and sometimes ask about outstanding debt, judgments, wage garnishments, or past bankruptcy. Financial trouble is common and rarely disqualifying on its own. What we look for is whether your finances create a vulnerability to bribery, theft, or off-duty employment conflicts, and whether you're managing the situation responsibly — a payment plan looks very different from ignored collections and defaulted accounts.

Research note: Consumer Financial Protection Bureau guidance on employment background reports and Fair Credit Reporting Act applicant rights.

If an agency or employer obtains an employment background report from a consumer-reporting company, federal law generally requires your written permission. If information in that report may lead to an adverse hiring decision, you generally must receive a copy of the report and a summary of your rights before the decision becomes final, followed by an adverse-action notice if the decision is made. Use that opportunity to identify mistaken identity, duplicate records, incorrect case dispositions, or other factual errors. It is not a way to argue away accurate information or bypass the investigator's process. Government investigations conducted directly by an agency may involve different procedures, and state law may provide additional protections.

Criminal and driving history

Adult criminal convictions are evaluated against your agency's statutory and policy disqualifiers, which vary significantly by state and department — ask your recruiter directly what applies to you rather than assuming. Driving history matters more than applicants expect, since officers spend enormous time behind the wheel, often in pursuit or emergency-response conditions; a pattern of moving violations, at-fault collisions, or license suspensions will draw real scrutiny even without a single disqualifying incident.

Social media and digital footprint

Assume your public and semi-public content will be reviewed, and in many agencies this now includes a formal social media questionnaire on the PHS itself, asking you to list current and former usernames/handles. Investigators are typically looking for evidence of bias, extremism, excessive substance use, violent or degrading content, or material inconsistent with the values of the badge — not for occasional, lawful personal opinions.

- Review your own accounts as though a stranger were seeing them for the first time, including old posts, tagged photos, and group memberships.
- Don't delete everything right before applying — a suspiciously scrubbed account draws its own questions, and forensic tools can sometimes still find cached

content. Instead, going forward, post the way you'd want a professional colleague to see you.

Common reasons candidates are disqualified

- Deception or significant omission discovered during the background process — by far the most common reason, more common than any single underlying fact being disclosed.
- A documented pattern of integrity violations (theft, cheating, falsifying records) rather than an isolated youthful mistake.
- Recent or ongoing illegal drug use inconsistent with your agency's lookback policy.
- Termination for cause involving dishonesty, violence, or theft.
- A pattern of poor judgment or escalation in personal conflicts (restraining orders, repeated physical altercations, harassment complaints).

> *I can work with almost anything a candidate is upfront about. What I can't work with is being surprised.*

National Context: What Background Investigators Commonly Assess

Research note: California POST Regulation 1953 / Background Investigation Dimensions are used here as one detailed state example; agency and state frameworks differ.

A useful way to understand the background phase is to focus on patterns of behavior rather than searching for a single 'gotcha' fact. California POST publicly organizes its background framework around ten job-related dimensions, including integrity, safety/impulse control, risk-taking and substance-related behavior, stress and adversity, conscientiousness, interpersonal conduct, judgment, learning, and communication. Those category names are summarized here for orientation; the discussion and applicant guidance in this book are independent explanations, and other jurisdictions may use different frameworks.

The issue is usually pattern + recency + seriousness + candor + evidence of change

A single event rarely tells an investigator everything. The practical questions are often: How serious was it? How long ago? Was it repeated? Was anyone harmed? Did you accept responsibility? Did you comply with court/employer requirements? Is there a documented change in behavior? And—critically—did you disclose it accurately when asked?

Build your "master timeline" before the PHS

Create one private reference document for your own use. Include month/year for residences, roommates, jobs, supervisors, schools, citations/collisions, military assignments if applicable, relationships requested by the form, legal matters, and prior public-safety applications. Use records to resolve uncertainty instead of guessing. Update the timeline when you discover a correction and follow the agency's instructions for amendments.

Prior applications and background files

Expect agencies to ask where else you have applied and whether you were rejected, withdrawn, non-selected or disqualified. Definitions vary. Answer the wording actually used. If a prior agency allows you to obtain records, those records may help you reconcile dates and disclosures—but never assume you are entitled to confidential investigative material.

How to write a clean disclosure explanation

Element	What to include
What happened	Plain facts without euphemisms, excuses or unnecessary drama.
When / how often	Best-supported date range and frequency; say when an estimate is an estimate.
Your responsibility	What you personally did or failed to do.
Outcome	Court/employer/school/DMV result, if any, and whether obligations were completed.
Change since	Concrete behavior change, time elapsed, treatment/education if relevant and appropriate, improved habits or record.
Documentation	Disposition, receipt, policy, transcript, driving record or other record when requested and lawfully available.

Do not "self-disqualify" from internet folklore
State law, POST/licensing rules, and local policy vary. If your history may be an issue, read the actual agency standard and ask recruiting/background staff what must be disclosed. Do not rely on an anonymous forum post from another state or another decade.

Background Investigation Deep Dive

This is where your isolated answers become a record. When I review a file, I am not simply reading your PHS from top to bottom. I am comparing dates, documents, interviews, references, prior applications, and other authorized sources to determine whether the overall history is complete, internally consistent, and suitable under the hiring agency's standards.

California POST is a useful public example of how formal this process can be. Its current standards require the POST background dimensions to be considered in every California peace-officer background investigation, and the current POST manual describes the PHS as a foundational source for the investigation. Other states and agencies use different forms and standards, so always follow the instructions of the agency to which you applied.

Source note: California POST, Peace Officer Candidate Selection Standards; Background Investigation Manual - Guidelines for the Investigator (revised December 2025). Summarized and paraphrased; California requirements are used as a public example, not as nationwide rules.

The PHS Is a Starting Point, Not a Memory Test

You may feel as though the PHS expects you to remember every date, address, supervisor, citation, roommate, and event in one sitting. It does not. I want you to reconstruct your history from reliable records before you begin the official form.

Build a month-and-year timeline of residences, employment, school, military service if applicable, and periods of unemployment.

Compare your timeline against tax records, resumes, transcripts, leases, old calendars, email, driving records, and other lawful records available to you.

Identify gaps before submission. A gap is a prompt to research your own history, not a reason to invent a date.

When the form permits estimates, identify them honestly as estimates. When it requires exact information, make a reasonable effort to obtain the record.

Keep a working copy of the information you submitted when agency rules permit it, and update your private timeline when your circumstances change.

Investigator's perspective: A candidate who says, 'I do not remember the exact day, but my records place it in March 2021,' is giving the investigator something that can be evaluated. A candidate who invents an exact date to make the form look complete creates a different problem: false precision.

The Background Interview: Where the File Becomes a Conversation

When you sit down with your investigator, do not expect a simple rereading of the PHS. I use that conversation to clarify chronology, ask about discrepancies, obtain context, identify additional sources, and give you an opportunity to correct or expand information. The tone may be conversational, but the information matters.

Before the interview

Review the information you actually submitted; do not memorize a polished version of it.

Bring only documents the investigator requested.

Write down newly remembered information or discovered errors so you do not forget to raise them.

Be ready to explain gaps, unusual transitions, discipline, terminations, prior applications, legal events, and other matters the agency asks about.

If you do not understand a question, ask what the investigator means before answering.

During the interview

Listen to the entire question. Answer the question asked, then provide relevant context. Do not bury a difficult fact inside a long explanation. A useful sequence is: state what happened, accept your role where appropriate, explain the outcome, and identify what changed. Context can matter; excuses and blame-shifting usually make context harder to evaluate.

Key principle: The goal is not to sound perfect. The goal is to make the investigator's file more accurate.

When Your Information Conflicts With a Record

Conflicts are not all equal. A date that is off by one month is different from an undisclosed termination. A former supervisor's opinion is different from an official disciplinary record. An investigator considers the nature of the conflict, the reliability of each source, whether the discrepancy is material, and how the applicant responds when it is raised.

Do not immediately accuse the source of lying simply because the information is unfavorable.

Separate factual disagreement from opinion. 'I was terminated on May 4' is a factual claim; 'he was difficult to supervise' is an opinion.

If your earlier answer was wrong, correct it directly.

If you have documentation that genuinely clarifies the issue, offer it through the investigator's requested process.

If you do not know why two records differ, say that. Do not manufacture an explanation.

Omissions, Corrections, and the Moment You Remember Something

One of the most important applicant decisions occurs after submission: you remember something you should have included. The instinct to stay quiet because 'it is already submitted' can turn an ordinary correction into an integrity concern. The better response is to learn the agency's correction procedure and address the issue promptly.

A clean correction should answer four questions:

What information was incomplete or inaccurate?

What is the correct information?

Why was the original answer incomplete or inaccurate, if you know?

When did you recognize the problem and what did you do to correct it?

Do not over-engineer the explanation: If you forgot, say you forgot. If you misunderstood the question, explain the misunderstanding. If you were embarrassed and intentionally omitted something, honesty requires acknowledging that too. The correction does not erase the original decision, but continuing the omission compounds it.

Once the process begins, preserve rather than sanitize. Do not delete accounts, posts, messages, documents, or other material to conceal your history. Keep a private working copy of what you submitted, update your timeline when your circumstances change, and report a new citation, police contact, address, job, or other material event when the agency instructs you to do so. If you discover an error, use the agency's correction process promptly and keep a copy of the correction for your records.

Prior Applications and Previous Background Investigations

Prior law-enforcement applications deserve their own preparation file. Agencies may ask where you applied, what stage you reached, whether you withdrew, were non-selected, were disqualified, or received another disposition. Use the exact terminology you were given rather than converting every unsuccessful process into 'I failed the background.'

Create a chronological list of every agency and position requested by the current form.

Record approximate application dates, stages reached, investigator/examiner names if known, and the disposition you were actually told.

Preserve correspondence that documents withdrawals, non-selections, conditional offers, or disqualifications.

If you do not know why an agency ended your process, do not invent a reason.

Expect a new investigator to compare what you say now with information lawfully available from prior processes.

Employment History: More Than Dates and Job Titles

Employment contacts can reveal patterns that a resume never shows: attendance, reliability, conflict, discipline, honesty, judgment, response to supervision, and eligibility for rehire. Applicants should prepare for employment verification by knowing their own history, not by attempting to influence what a former employer will say.

Issues that deserve advance self-review

Terminations, resignations under pressure, or resignations during an investigation.

Written discipline, performance improvement plans, attendance problems, or policy violations.

Conflicts with supervisors or coworkers that generated formal complaints.

Unreported side jobs, periods of unemployment, or overlapping employment dates.

Any occasion on which you were accused of dishonesty, theft, falsification, harassment, violence, or misuse of confidential information.

Applicant strategy: Know the facts, disclose what the form requires, and resist the urge to pre-argue the case. The investigator can obtain both sides.

Financial History: Distinguishing Hardship From Conduct

Financial difficulty is not the same thing as financial irresponsibility. Job loss, medical bills, divorce, family obligations, or a failed business can create legitimate hardship. Investigators may be interested in the applicant's conduct around the problem: avoidance, dishonesty, repeated preventable behavior, unresolved legal obligations, or evidence of responsible efforts to address the issue.

Know what is currently delinquent and why.

Keep documentation of payment plans, settlements, satisfied judgments, or disputes when relevant.

Do not claim an account is 'taken care of' if you have only stopped receiving calls.

If an account is disputed, distinguish 'I dispute this debt' from 'this debt does not exist.'

Answer the agency's actual questions; financial screening practices and legal requirements vary.

Criminal, Driving, Drug, and Other Conduct: Read the Question Literally

Applicants frequently make disclosure errors by answering the question they wish had been asked. A form may distinguish arrests, detentions, citations, convictions, diversion, juvenile conduct, civil restraining orders, license suspensions, collisions, illegal drug use, prescription misuse, or other conduct. Those categories are not interchangeable.

Do not rely on a friend's hiring experience or an internet list of 'automatic disqualifiers.' State law, agency policy, civil-service rules, and the age and nature of conduct can produce different outcomes. California POST itself notes that local agencies may impose standards above statewide minimums and that detection-of deception examinations can be locally required even though POST does not require them.

Criminal and Legal History

Prepare a lifetime inventory of law-enforcement contacts so you can answer the agency's exact questions completely. Do not limit your preparation to arrests or convictions.

- List every detention, investigative stop, field interview, citation, arrest, or other direct contact with a law-enforcement agency when the form asks for it, whether or not you were charged or the matter appears on a criminal-history record.
- Include law-enforcement responses to any residence where you lived when you were involved, identified, questioned, detained, cited, arrested, named in a report, or otherwise asked about by the form. Distinguish your role accurately - reporting party, victim, witness, subject, suspect, or another role.
- Identify every police report you filed or caused to be filed and what it concerned, including theft, fraud, collision, lost property, threats, domestic incidents, vandalism, or another reported event. Record the agency, approximate date, report number if available, and outcome.
- Include juvenile matters, sealed or expunged matters, diversion, restraining-order proceedings, and other contacts only as the agency question and applicable law require. Never decide on your own that a matter no longer counts.

Driving History

Prepare a complete lifetime driving history before you begin the PHS. That master list should include:

- Every moving or equipment citation you have ever received, including fix-it citations and citations later dismissed, corrected, reduced, or kept off the public driving record after traffic school. Do not include ordinary parking citations unless the agency specifically asks for them.
- Every motor-vehicle collision or accident in which you were the driver, not merely a passenger. Include events where a law-enforcement agency made a report, the drivers only exchanged information, or the event was not formally reported but a vehicle or someone else's property was damaged.
- For each collision, record the approximate date and location, vehicles or property involved, injuries if any, whether information was exchanged, whether law enforcement responded, the report or case number if known, insurance disposition, citations, and your best factual description of responsibility.
- Every driver-license suspension, revocation, restriction, denial, or reinstatement, including the issuing jurisdiction, dates, reason, and how the matter was resolved.

From the Background Investigator's Desk: Traffic school, a corrected equipment violation, an unreported collision, or a later dismissal may affect what appears on a current record, but it does not erase the underlying event from your history. Reconstruct the facts and answer the wording on the agency's form.

Source note: California POST, Peace Officer Local Agency Policy and Candidate Selection Process. Local standards can exceed POST minimums; applicants should obtain agency-specific requirements.

Social Media and Digital History

Digital review has become more formalized in some background processes. California POST's December 2025 revision to its Background Investigation Manual added guidance for gathering social-media information, including legal considerations, information sources, sample questions, and documentation requirements. That is a useful signal to applicants: online conduct can be part of a modern suitability investigation, but the scope and method depend on the agency and law.

Prepare a lifetime account-and-address inventory before completing the PHS:

- List every social-media, messaging, forum, gaming, dating, video, photo-sharing, or other online account you have ever maintained when the form requests social-media or online identifiers. Include inactive, abandoned, suspended, deleted, renamed, and duplicate accounts - not only the accounts you currently use.
- Record every username, screen name, handle, display name, profile URL, and prior name associated with each account to the extent the form requests and you can reasonably reconstruct it.
- List every email address you have ever used, including old school or work addresses, abandoned personal addresses, aliases, and an address created only to open or verify a social-media or online account.
- Do not reactivate, delete, alter, or conceal accounts merely to influence the investigation. Follow the agency's instructions and identify uncertainty honestly when an old username or address cannot be recovered.

Source note: California POST December 2025 Report and Background Investigation Manual revision. Paraphrased.

Review what is publicly associated with your name and known usernames so you are not surprised by your own history.

Do not fabricate a new online identity for the hiring process.

Do not pressure friends to delete posts or conceal relevant information.

If the PHS asks for usernames or accounts, follow its instructions rather than deciding for yourself which accounts 'count.'

How Investigators Reconcile Conflicting Information

Background work is an exercise in corroboration. No single reference, record, interview, or database entry automatically tells the whole story. The investigator looks for convergence: independent sources pointing toward the same conclusion, or a pattern of inconsistencies that requires explanation.

A practical credibility framework

Specificity: Does the source describe concrete events or only broad impressions?

Proximity: Did the source personally observe the event or hear about it from someone else?

Contemporaneous records: Are there documents created near the time of the event?

Consistency: Does the account remain materially stable when details are checked?

Bias and relationship: Does the source have a reason to exaggerate, minimize, protect, or retaliate?

Corroboration: Do independent sources support or contradict the account?

Applicant response: Does the applicant address the issue directly, or does the explanation change as new information appears?

Important: This framework is not a formula that applicants can game. It explains why complete disclosure matters: investigators rarely rely on only one piece of information.

From the Investigator's Desk: Case Studies

The following scenarios are composites created for education. They are not descriptions of identifiable applicants or cases. They illustrate how ordinary facts can become more significant when information is omitted, minimized, or contradicted.

Case 1 - The 'Voluntary' Resignation

Scenario: The applicant lists a prior employer and writes 'resigned for a better opportunity.' The employer reports that the applicant resigned after being told a disciplinary investigation was likely.

What the investigator examines: The issue is not automatically the workplace allegation. The investigator now has to determine whether the applicant's description was materially incomplete and what the applicant knew when completing the PHS.

Applicant lesson: Disclose the circumstances when the form asks about discipline, investigations, forced resignations, or reasons for leaving, and explain the outcome accurately.

Case 2 - The Forgotten Prior Application

Scenario: An applicant reports three prior police applications. A records request reveals a fourth application several years earlier that reached the background stage.

What the investigator examines: A forgotten online interest form may be understandable; forgetting a completed background process is harder to reconcile. The surrounding facts matter.

Applicant lesson: Maintain a prior-application log and correct omissions as soon as you discover them.

Case 3 - The Negative Former Roommate

Scenario: A former roommate describes the applicant as argumentative during a difficult year and reports several loud disputes. Other contacts describe the applicant as calm and responsible.

What the investigator examines: One negative source does not automatically decide suitability. The investigator evaluates specificity, timing, corroboration, bias, and whether the applicant disclosed relevant incidents.

Applicant lesson: Do not try to remove every critical person from the investigator's reach. Give accurate history and context.

Case 4 - The Date Discrepancy

Scenario: The PHS says employment ended in June; payroll records show the final paid day in May and a separation date in early June.

What the investigator examines: This may be a normal record-definition issue rather than deception. The investigator asks which date the applicant was using and whether the discrepancy changes anything material.

Applicant lesson: Do not invent exact dates. Use records and identify estimates when allowed.

Case 5 - The Debt That Was 'Handled'

Scenario: The applicant says an old account was resolved. A current record shows an unpaid collection.

What the investigator examines: The investigator needs to know whether the applicant misunderstood the account status, disputed it, forgot it, or knowingly minimized it.

Applicant lesson: Know the actual status and bring relevant documentation if requested.

Case 6 - The Late Disclosure

Scenario: After submitting the PHS, the applicant remembers an incident that should have been listed and waits until the investigator asks about it.

What the investigator examines: The underlying event and the delay become separate issues. The investigator may ask when the applicant remembered and why the applicant did not correct the form.

Applicant lesson: Prompt correction is generally more defensible than hoping the issue never appears.

Case 7 - The Reference Who Adds a New Topic

Scenario: A listed reference tells the investigator about a period of heavy drinking that the applicant did not believe was worth mentioning.

What the investigator examines: The investigator returns to the exact wording of the PHS and prior interview. Was the subject asked? If so, was the answer complete?

Applicant lesson: Do not decide that a fact is irrelevant when the official question requires it.

Case 8 - The Applicant Who Over-Explains

Scenario: Every difficult event is followed by a long explanation assigning responsibility to supervisors, friends, former partners, or circumstances.

What the investigator examines: Even when individual explanations are plausible, a repeated inability to identify one's own role can become relevant to judgment, accountability, and interpersonal functioning.

Applicant lesson: Context matters, but accountability makes context credible.

Background Readiness Self-Assessment

Before beginning a background process, ask yourself whether you can answer yes to each statement:

I have reconstructed the residences, jobs, schools, and major events required by the agency's lookback periods.

I know how to contact former employers, supervisors, roommates, and references requested by the form.

I have reviewed my prior law-enforcement applications and can describe their outcomes accurately.

I have identified legal, driving, financial, drug/alcohol, employment, and disciplinary issues that the agency may ask about.

I am prepared to disclose embarrassing information rather than gamble that it will not be discovered.

I understand that a correction after submission should be made through the agency's process.

I can distinguish facts I know from dates/details I am estimating.

I am prepared for the investigator to speak with people I did not select.

I am willing to accept responsibility for my conduct without rewriting my history.

I understand that suitability standards vary and that the hiring agency - not this book - makes the decision.

The Standard to Carry Into Every Stage

The strongest preparation strategy is remarkably consistent from the PHS through the background interview, collateral contacts, polygraph or CVSA where used, psychological evaluation, and final review: know your own history, answer the question asked, correct errors, provide records when requested, and tell the truth even when the truthful answer is uncomfortable.

Organization can improve your file. Preparation can improve your communication. Experience can help you understand what investigators are looking at. None of those things should be used to manufacture a different history. The purpose of this book is to help you present the real one completely and professionally.

The Applicant File Audit: Before You Press Submit

A final self-audit is one of the highest-value steps an applicant can take. It is not a search for ways to make the history look better. It is a search for omissions, contradictions, missing contact information, and answers that do not actually respond to the question asked.

Audit the chronology

Do residence dates leave unexplained gaps or overlaps?

Do employment dates align with the resume, tax records, and the master timeline?

Are periods of unemployment, school, military service, travel, or caregiving accounted for where the form requires them?

Have you used the same legal names, former names, and aliases wherever the form requires them?

Audit the people

Are supervisor, coworker, roommate, landlord, neighbor, and reference contacts current to the extent you can reasonably verify them?

Did you accidentally use the same person in multiple categories when the form asks for different relationships?

Did you omit someone because the relationship ended badly rather than because the form excludes that person?

Have you warned listed contacts only that they may be contacted - without coaching them about what to say?

Audit the disclosures

Read each disclosure question literally and compare it with your private history notes.

Check whether the question asks about conduct rather than only arrests, convictions, discipline, or formal findings.

Look for answers that rely on vague phrases such as 'nothing serious,' 'handled,' or 'a long time ago.' Replace vagueness with responsive facts when the form calls for them.

Identify any answer you would be uncomfortable explaining if an investigator placed a contradictory record beside it. Recheck that answer now.

Submission rule: Accuracy first, appearance second. A complete answer that requires explanation is safer than an attractive answer that becomes incomplete when verified.

What Happens When an Investigator Calls You Back

Follow-up contact is normal. A request for clarification does not necessarily mean the investigator has concluded that you lied or that you are about to be disqualified. Background investigations generate loose ends: dates differ, employers use different terminology, references remember events differently, and records sometimes require explanation.

When you receive a follow-up request

Write down exactly what the investigator is requesting and the deadline.

Answer the question actually asked before adding background information.

If the investigator requests a record, obtain the record rather than substituting your recollection when reasonably possible.

If your earlier statement was wrong, say so plainly and correct it.

If you need time to verify a fact, ask whether you may confirm it rather than guessing.

Keep the investigator informed if a third party or records custodian is causing a delay.

The danger of the moving explanation

A difficult fact does not become easier to evaluate when the explanation changes every time a new record appears. Sometimes a changing explanation is innocent - the applicant learns new information or remembers more detail. If that happens, identify what changed and why. What damages credibility is silently replacing one version with another as though the earlier version never existed.

Professional habit: Treat every correction as part of the record. 'I previously told you X. I reviewed the document you requested and learned the correct information is Y' is clearer than pretending X was never said.

Four More Investigator Case Studies

Case 9 - The Supervisor Who Will Not Respond

Scenario: The applicant repeatedly contacts a former supervisor and becomes frustrated when the supervisor ignores the investigator.

What the investigator examines: A nonresponsive source is an investigative problem for the investigator to manage, not permission for the applicant to pressure or script the source.

Applicant lesson: Provide updated contact information when requested, identify legitimate alternate contacts if permitted, and let the investigator decide how to proceed.

Case 10 - The 'It Was Expunged' Assumption

Scenario: An applicant leaves an event off because a court process later changed the public record status.

What the investigator examines: Whether an event must be disclosed depends on the exact question, applicable law, and agency instructions. The applicant's assumption may not match what the form requires.

Applicant lesson: Read the question and instructions. If uncertain, seek clarification from the agency rather than making your own legal conclusion about disclosure.

Case 11 - The Social-Media Explanation

Scenario: An old post appears inconsistent with the applicant's current account of an event. The applicant immediately says the account must have been hacked.

What the investigator examines: The investigator may examine dates, surrounding posts, account history, other witnesses, and whether the explanation is supported by anything beyond the applicant's desire to distance themselves from the content.

Applicant lesson: Do not invent a technical explanation. If the post is yours, address it. If you genuinely believe it is not, explain why and provide legitimate supporting information if available.

Case 12 - The Honest but Uncertain Applicant

Scenario: The applicant is asked for the month of an event from many years earlier and cannot remember it. Records are unavailable.

What the investigator examines: Uncertainty is not automatically deception. The investigator can evaluate the applicant's effort to locate the information, the importance of the date, and whether other evidence narrows the timeframe.

Applicant lesson: Good-faith uncertainty should be identified as uncertainty when the form or investigator permits. Never turn 'I think' into 'I know' merely to make the answer look complete.

Investigator-Ready Document Index

Create a private index of records you have located. Do not send documents the agency has not requested; the purpose is to know what exists and where you can retrieve it.

Identity and eligibility records requested by the agency.

Education transcripts, diplomas, certifications, and credential evaluations if applicable.

Military service or discharge records if applicable.

Employment records in your possession, including discipline or separation documents relevant to questions asked.

Driving-history and court records you lawfully obtained.

Documents supporting resolution of financial matters when relevant.

Prior law-enforcement application correspondence and disposition notices.

Current contact list for references, supervisors, roommates, landlords, and other categories requested.

A discrepancy/correction log showing what you corrected, when, and how.

Do not create a massive unsolicited evidence dump. Organization is valuable because it lets you respond accurately and promptly when the investigator asks for something.

Chapter 5: Beyond Family and Bosses — Collateral and Peer References

This is one of the most misunderstood parts of the process, and it's worth its own chapter. Applicants often assume the reference section of the PHS is satisfied by listing a parent, a pastor, a current supervisor, and a college professor. Those references matter, but experienced investigators know exactly what they're worth: people in positions of authority or family loyalty toward you have every incentive to describe you favorably. That doesn't make them useless, but it does make them incomplete.

From the Background Investigator's Desk: Collateral contacts

Your references are starting points, not a boundary around the investigation. I may contact supervisors, coworkers, neighbors, roommates, former partners, or other people identified through authorized sources because a background is built through corroboration. Your job is to provide accurate contact information and appropriate notice when instructed. It is not to coach anyone, demand a favorable answer, or try to discover who said what.

Why we go looking for people you didn't list

What we're actually trying to find is how you behave when nobody grading you, employing you, raising you, or shepherding your soul is in the room. That's a genuinely different data set than 'how do you act at work' or 'how do you act at church' or 'how do you act around your mother.' It's how you act with a roommate splitting a utility bill at midnight, a teammate on a rec-league team after a bad call by the ref, a friend you've known for a decade who has seen you drink too much or go through a breakup, or a landlord who had to chase you for a late payment.

- Family members are asked and want to protect you — understandably.
- Supervisors are often coached, consciously or not, to give a neutral or positive reference to avoid liability, and they usually only see your 'work self.'
- School references (teachers, professors, coaches in an official capacity) usually only see a narrow, structured version of you.
- Clergy and mentors typically see the version of you that shows up specifically for that relationship.

None of that is dishonest on their part — it's simply the natural limit of what any single relationship can show. Peer and collateral references fill in the rest of the picture.

Who counts as a collateral or peer reference

These are people who knew you socially, informally, or in shared living/recreational situations — not because you were being evaluated, mentored, employed, or raised by them, but because you happened to share space, time, or an activity with them.

Category	Examples	What it reveals
Roommates / former roommates	College roommate, apartment co-tenant, former partner you lived with	Day-to-day honesty, shared responsibility, temper, cleanliness/reliability with shared obligations
Landlords / property managers	Current or past landlord, HOA contact	Payment reliability, respect for property and rules, how disputes were handled
Recreational/social circle	Rec-league teammates, gym regulars, hobby group members, gaming or hunting/fishing buddies	Sportsmanship, temper under competitive pressure, how you treat people with no stake in your career
Long-term friends outside work/family/church	Childhood or close adult friends not tied to your professional or family network	Consistency of character over time, how you handle friends' hardships, loyalty and honesty in private
Neighbors (informal)	People who lived next to you, not just a formal 'neighborhood check'	Noise, disputes, general conduct, how you treat people you didn't choose to be around
Former significant others	Ex-partners, particularly from longer relationships	Conflict resolution, temper, honesty, treatment of someone who owed you nothing
Volunteer or fraternal contacts outside religious settings	Civic clubs, sports coaching (volunteer, non-employment), community organizing	Follow-through on commitments with no supervisor enforcing them

What we actually ask these contacts

The questions are usually open-ended and behavioral, not yes/no, because we're listening for hesitation and specifics as much as content:

- How did you meet, and how well and how long have you known them?
- Have you ever seen them lose their temper? What happened?
- Have you ever seen them drink, and if so, how do they behave?
- Have you ever known them to lie to you or to someone else, even about something small?
- How do they handle owing someone money, or someone owing them?

- Have you ever seen them treat a service worker, a stranger, or someone who couldn't reciprocate poorly?
- Is there anything about their character that gives you pause about them carrying a badge and a gun?
- Is there anything you think I should ask them about directly?

That last question matters — a good collateral interview often surfaces a topic we then bring back to you directly, which is exactly why consistency across every conversation matters so much.

How applicants should approach this

- List a genuinely mixed reference set on your PHS: not just people who will flatter you, but people from different chapters of your life — a roommate, a teammate, a longtime friend, not only relatives, clergy, and supervisors.
- Tell the people you list that an investigator may call, so they aren't caught off guard and don't sound evasive simply from surprise.
- Don't try to control what they'll say. Coaching a reference on what to say (as opposed to simply giving them a heads-up) is itself a red flag investigators are trained to listen for.
- Expect that we may also talk to people you didn't list — a former roommate mentioned by someone else, a name that comes up in a neighbor interview. This is normal and not a sign you're under unusual suspicion.
- If you know an old friend or ex-partner might describe a rough patch honestly, disclose that context yourself first. An investigator who hears about a conflict from you before hearing about it from someone else reads it as maturity, not as a liability.

> *The reference that tells me the most is rarely the pastor or the boss. It's the old roommate who pauses for a second and then tells me the truth anyway.*

A note on fairness to former partners and roommates

If your list of collateral contacts might include a former significant other or a roommate you parted with on bad terms, you don't need to remove them from consideration — investigators are trained to weigh context, including relationship endings, and to distinguish an honest account of conflict from someone with an axe to grind. What matters most is that your own account of that relationship, given up front, matches what we hear independently.

Reference Management Without Coaching

Your job is to provide accurate contact information and a fair heads-up—not to rehearse answers with references. Tell them the agency or background vendor may contact them, ask them to respond promptly, and verify the best phone number and email. If they ask what to say, the safest answer is: "Tell the truth from your own experience."

When a reference does not respond

Do not panic or repeatedly pressure the person. Notify your investigator if the agency asks you to assist with updated contact information. Have backup contact methods where the form permits them. Never create a substitute reference or provide someone else's contact information without permission.

Chapter 6: Polygraph and CVSA - The Instrument, the Examiner, and Complete Honesty

Not every agency uses a polygraph, and some states restrict or prohibit its use in pre-employment screening, but where it's part of the process it typically covers the same topics as your PHS: criminal history, drug use, integrity, employment honesty, and honesty on your application. It is not designed to catch you in a trick — it is designed to confirm that what you wrote and said matches what actually happened.

From the CVSA Examiner's Chair

After 10 years as a CVSA examiner, my practical advice is simple: do not make the instrument the center of your attention. The instrument is one tool that assists the examiner. It does not independently know whether you are truthful, and an examiner's behavioral observations are not infallible proof of deception. The examiner considers your statements, changes or clarifications, consistency with earlier disclosures, the examination process, and other authorized investigative context. Your responsibility is not to beat or impress a machine. Your responsibility is to answer completely and correct the record when necessary.

How the exam typically unfolds

- Pre-test interview: the examiner reviews your PHS answers with you verbally, topic by topic, and clarifies anything ambiguous.
- Question review: you'll see the exact relevant questions before you're connected to the instrument — nothing is sprung on you.
- The instrument phase: a series of short, direct yes/no questions repeated across a few charts.
- Post-test interview: if there's a reaction on a specific question, the examiner will usually ask you about it directly and give you a chance to explain before drawing conclusions.

Preparing for the polygraph

- Review your PHS again the night before so your memory of dates and details is fresh and consistent with what you already disclosed.
- Get a normal night's sleep and eat normally — being exhausted, dehydrated, or over-caffeinated affects your physiological baseline, not just your nerves.
- Answer the pre-test interview questions the same way, every time, without exaggerating or minimizing either direction.

- If something on your PHS is bothering you, raise it with the examiner or your investigator before the exam, not during it.
- Avoid trying any 'countermeasure' technique you've read about online — modern examiners are trained to recognize them, and being caught using one is treated as an independent integrity issue.

Candidates sometimes ask if there's a way to 'beat' the test. There isn't a reliable one, and trying tends to produce exactly the inconsistent, evasive pattern examiners are trained to notice. The far more effective strategy is simply making sure there's nothing left unsaid by the time you sit down.

What Detection-of-Deception Testing Can and Cannot Mean

There is no single national requirement that every police applicant take a polygraph. Some public agencies use polygraph or other detection-of-deception examinations; others do not, and state law can affect what is permitted. The federal Employee Polygraph Protection Act generally restricts most private employers, but federal, state and local government employers are excluded from that Act's coverage. That federal exclusion does not override state or local restrictions.

Preparation that is legitimate

Review your own application and PHS for completeness; make corrections through the agency's process; sleep normally; eat normally unless instructed otherwise; bring required identification; disclose medications or medical issues only as the agency/examiner instructs; and answer the question asked. Do not study or practice countermeasures.

Consistency does not mean memorization
An honest person may remember a date more precisely later. If new information changes an earlier estimate, explain the correction rather than forcing yourself to repeat an answer you now believe is inaccurate.

Detection-of-deception examinations are among the most misunderstood stages of a peace-officer hiring process. Some agencies use a conventional polygraph, some use Computer Voice Stress Analysis (CVSA) or another voice-stress system, and some use neither. The agency's rules, state law, and local policy control. Whatever instrument is used, the applicant should understand one point from the beginning: the instrument is a tool that assists the examiner. It is not a machine that literally reads truth from the human body or voice.

FROM THE EXAMINER'S CHAIR
The author brings 10 years of experience as a CVSA examiner in addition to 15 years conducting background investigations. The professional observations in this chapter are identified as examiner/investigator perspective and are kept separate from published scientific findings.

Why agencies use detection-of-deception examinations

In a pre-employment background process, the examination can serve several functions at once. It can focus an applicant on areas that require complete disclosure, give the examiner an organized opportunity to review potentially significant conduct, identify statements that require clarification, and provide information that can be compared with the PHS, background interview, records, and collateral information. Those investigative functions should not be confused with a claim that any instrument is infallible.

The federal Employee Polygraph Protection Act generally restricts lie-detector testing by most private employers. Federal, state, and local government employers are excluded from that federal law's coverage, although state and local law and agency policy can impose their own restrictions. The Department of Labor's definition of a lie detector expressly includes polygraphs and voice-stress analyzers.

Source note: U.S. Department of Labor, Fact Sheet #36, Employee Polygraph Protection Act. Government employers are excluded from EPPA coverage; state/local restrictions may still apply.

Polygraph and CVSA: different instruments, different signals

A conventional polygraph records several physiological channels at the same time. Federal law describes minimum polygraph instrumentation as continuously recording cardiovascular, respiratory, and electrodermal patterns. The examiner evaluates recorded responses within the examination protocol; the instrument itself does not directly record a variable called 'truth' or 'deception.'

CVSA works differently. It analyzes characteristics of the examinee's recorded voice rather than simultaneously collecting the cardiovascular, respiratory, and electrodermal channels used by a conventional polygraph. The practical experience of sitting for the two examinations can therefore differ substantially even when the agency is using either examination to explore similar integrity and background topics.

Feature	Polygraph	CVSA / voice stress
Primary input	Multiple physiological channels recorded through attached sensors	Recorded spoken responses analyzed by voice-stress software
Applicant connection	Sensors are physically attached during chart collection	Typically uses a microphone / recorded voice rather than polygraph sensor array
Examiner role	Pre-test review, question formulation, chart collection, interpretation, follow-up	Pre-test review, question formulation, voice collection, interpretation, follow-up

Feature	Polygraph	CVSA / voice stress
What it does not do	Does not directly measure a variable called a lie	Does not directly measure a variable called a lie
Scientific literature	Substantial literature; accuracy varies by method and application and is not perfect	Independent studies cited below have reported serious limitations in deception-detection performance
Applicant strategy	Complete, candid answers and compliance with instructions	Complete, candid answers and compliance with instructions

What the science says - and why the book will not oversell either instrument

Scientific evidence should be discussed separately from an examiner's professional experience. Polygraph research is not accurately summarized by saying either 'it always works' or 'it is worthless.' The National Academies concluded that specific-incident polygraph testing can discriminate lying from truth telling at rates above chance but well below perfection, and warned that screening applications present additional difficulties. That distinction matters in employment screening, where the examiner is often addressing broad historical topics rather than one known event.

Independent research on voice-stress analysis has been more critical. An NIJ-sponsored field study evaluating CVSA and another voice-stress system in a jail setting found that the systems did not detect deception about recent drug use better than chance in that study and reported poor reliability between some expert and novice interpretations. A separate published evaluation of the NITV CVSA using laboratory and field speech databases likewise reported performance near chance for the databases studied.

These findings do not erase the practical fact that an examination may generate useful investigative information. They do require us to distinguish two questions: 'How scientifically accurate is the instrument at classifying deception?' and 'Can the examination process help an examiner obtain disclosures, clarify inconsistencies, or identify matters requiring investigation?' Those are not the same question.

Source note: National Research Council, The Polygraph and Lie Detection (2003); National Institute of Justice / Office of Justice Programs, Assessing the Validity of Voice Stress Analysis Tools in a Jail Setting (2007); Hollien et al., Evaluation of the NITV CVSA, Journal of Forensic Sciences (2008). Findings are summarized and paraphrased.

The instrument is a tool - not the examiner

From the author's examiner and investigator perspective, the instrument should assist professional judgment rather than replace it. An experienced examiner is evaluating more than a chart or software display: the applicant's answers, disclosures, clarifications, consistency with information already supplied, changes in the account, and the context in which those responses occur. In a background investigation, relevant information may then be compared with records and other authorized investigative sources.

Experience with applicant behavior is an important part of deciding what deserves follow-up, but behavior is not an infallible truth meter. Nervousness, hesitation, discomfort, poor memory, eye contact, or an unusual mannerism cannot by themselves prove deception. The experienced examiner's advantage is not a magical ability to read a person; it is the ability to recognize when an answer, pattern, inconsistency, or disclosure warrants a better question or additional verification.

THE PRACTICAL LITMUS TEST

In the author's professional practice, experience with applicant behavior is a critical credibility-assessment tool. The safest way to express that principle is that behavior guides questioning and verification; it does not replace corroboration. Instrument data, applicant statements, examiner observations, and the broader investigation should be considered together.

The pre-examination questionnaire: a roadmap, not a study guide

Many agencies or examiners use a written pre-polygraph, pre-CVSA, or detection-of-deception questionnaire. The exact form and terminology vary. Treat it as part of the examination process, not as disposable paperwork. Read every question carefully, answer completely, and follow the examiner's or agency's instructions.

The questionnaire is also a good indication of where discussion may go. If it asks about drug use, theft, criminal conduct, falsification, workplace misconduct, prior applications, undisclosed contacts with law enforcement, or another integrity topic, it is reasonable to expect that an answer in that area may be reviewed or clarified during the pre-test interview or examination process. That is useful preparation information - but it is not an invitation to predict exact test questions or rehearse a response designed to produce a particular result.

Use the questionnaire to ask yourself a different question: 'Have I disclosed everything this question requires?' If it causes you to remember information that was missing or inaccurate on your application or PHS, address the discrepancy through the process the agency provides. Do not hope that the examiner will simply miss it.

CONSISTENCY THROUGH TRUTHFULNESS

PHS -> pre-examination questionnaire -> pre-test interview -> instrument phase -> clarification/follow-up -> background investigation. Information may be revisited at multiple points. The goal is not memorized consistency. It is consistency that naturally follows from complete, truthful disclosure.

The pre-test interview

The pre-test phase is often the most important part for the applicant to understand. The examiner reviews the relevant subject areas, resolves ambiguity, establishes what particular words or time periods mean, and gives the applicant an opportunity to clarify answers. Where a formal questionnaire is used, it can organize much of this discussion.

This is also where applicants sometimes create unnecessary problems by trying to decide which version of an answer 'sounds best.' If a question is unclear, ask for clarification. If your memory is uncertain, say so. If an earlier answer was wrong, correct it. An examiner cannot evaluate information you deliberately keep off the table.

Question review and the instrument phase

Protocols differ, so applicants should not assume that every examiner or agency follows one universal script. In many structured examinations, the examiner reviews the questions or their meaning before collecting the instrument data. The instrument phase then consists of controlled question sequences administered according to the examiner's protocol. Follow instructions exactly and answer the question that is asked rather than volunteering a speech during a yes/no sequence unless the examiner requests explanation.

This book intentionally does not reproduce proprietary question sets, scoring rules, chart examples, software screens, or countermeasure material. Applicants do not need that information to prepare honestly, and attempting to manipulate breathing, movement, voice, mental activity, or other responses can create a separate integrity concern.

Nervousness, reactions, and inconclusive results

Being nervous is not the same thing as lying. Police applicants can be anxious because the job matters, the environment is unfamiliar, or they fear being misunderstood. Physiological arousal and vocal changes can have causes other than deception. That is one reason responsible interpretation cannot be reduced to 'the machine reacted, therefore the applicant lied.'

Likewise, a result described as inconclusive or requiring additional review is not automatically a finding of deception. Terminology and procedures vary by system and agency. The appropriate applicant response is to follow instructions, answer follow-up questions candidly, and provide any requested clarification or documentation.

Admissions and clarifications

A significant practical value of the examination process can occur before or after the instrument records anything: an applicant remembers something, recognizes that a prior answer was incomplete, or finally discloses conduct that should have been reported earlier. From a background-investigation perspective, the newly disclosed conduct and the delay in disclosing it may be separate issues. The examiner does not decide that distinction for every agency; the hiring authority evaluates the information under its standards.

Do not assume that admitting an uncomfortable fact automatically ends your candidacy, and do not assume that withholding it protects you. The seriousness, recency, frequency, surrounding circumstances, agency standards, and your candor can all matter. What you control is whether your account is complete and truthful.

Complete honesty is the only preparation strategy this book recommends

There is no responsible technique this book can give you that guarantees you will 'pass' a polygraph or CVSA. Neither instrument is scientifically infallible, and complete honesty cannot guarantee a particular instrument classification. But honesty is the one part of the process fully within your control, and it is the only preparation strategy consistent with the integrity expected of a peace-officer applicant.

Do not try to beat the instrument or research countermeasures.

Do not change an answer because you think a different answer will look better on the chart or screen.

Do not minimize frequency, recency, amount, or your own role in an event.

Do not invent precision when you genuinely do not remember a date or detail.

Do correct an inaccurate prior disclosure through the agency's process.

Do ask for clarification when you do not understand a question.

Do answer completely and truthfully, then let the examiner do the examiner's job.

THE BOTTOM LINE
Your job is not to 'pass the machine.' Your job is to tell the truth. The instrument assists the examiner; the examiner's experience guides questioning and interpretation; and the background investigation supplies the broader context. Complete honesty gives the process the best information available and prevents an applicant from creating a new integrity problem through concealment or manipulation.

Applicant self-review before the examination

Re-read the agency's instructions and any questionnaire you are required to complete.

Review your own PHS/application for accuracy - not to memorize wording.

Identify anything you now believe is incomplete or incorrect and learn how the agency wants corrections submitted.

Bring only documents or identification requested by the agency/examiner.

Sleep and eat normally unless the agency gives different instructions.

Follow instructions regarding medications or medical issues; do not stop prescribed medication merely to affect an examination without guidance from the prescribing clinician.

Arrive prepared to discuss uncomfortable subjects candidly.

Do not practice countermeasures, scripted denials, or behavioral tricks.

Chapter 7: The Psychological Evaluation

This stage usually has two parts: a standardized written personality inventory (commonly the MMPI-2-RF or a similar instrument, sometimes paired with the CPI, PAI, or an IPI) and a one-on-one interview with a licensed psychologist familiar with public-safety selection.

A direct word about psychological screening

I know why applicants become anxious here. You may worry that one answer will define you or that counseling automatically disqualifies you. Do not diagnose yourself from an internet forum and do not try to manufacture an ideal personality. Read carefully, answer honestly, and let the licensed evaluator apply the agency's job-related standards. My observations about applicant preparation are not psychological advice; the sourced standards and the evaluator's professional judgment control.

The written inventory

- Answer honestly and consistently — these instruments include built-in validity scales that flag inconsistent, random, or overly 'good' answer patterns, and an inflated profile can be as concerning to an evaluator as a troubling one.
- Don't try to guess the 'correct' personality profile. The psychologist is looking for stability, impulse control, and sound judgment under stress, not a specific personality type.
- Take the inventory when you're rested and unhurried — rushing through hundreds of true/false items tends to produce a less reliable, less representative profile.

The clinical interview

- Expect direct questions about stress, anger, family history, past hardship, and substance use. Evaluators expect candidates to have faced real adversity; what matters is how you coped with it.
- Answer questions about your PHS disclosures consistently with what you've already told your background investigator — this is another cross-check point.
- Get a normal amount of sleep beforehand and avoid presenting an overly polished, rehearsed version of yourself — evaluators are experienced at noticing when answers feel scripted rather than genuine.
- If you have a history of counseling or a mental health diagnosis, disclose it if asked. A disclosed, well-managed history is treated very differently than an evasive non-answer that's later discovered.

What the Psychological Evaluation Is Designed to Assess

Research note: California POST Psychological Screening Manual and selection standards; federal ADA/EEOC guidance for timing/confidentiality.

Public-safety psychological screening evaluates job-related suitability rather than searching for one ideal 'police personality.' Procedures vary, but they may combine standardized psychological instruments, relevant history, and a clinical interview. California POST's published standards are one example of a jurisdiction requiring more than one written measure plus an interview; applicants elsewhere should verify the process used by their own agency.

Common job-related themes

Frameworks used in public-safety screening commonly examine areas such as social competence, teamwork, adaptability/flexibility, conscientiousness/dependability, impulse control, integrity/ethics, emotional regulation/stress tolerance, decision-making/judgment, assertiveness/persuasiveness, and substance-abuse or other risk-taking behavior. The specific dimensions and test instruments vary by agency and state.

How to approach the written instruments

Read each item carefully, answer it yourself, and avoid trying to reverse-engineer a “perfect officer” profile. Many standardized instruments contain validity indicators designed to detect inconsistent, random, exaggerated or unrealistically virtuous responding. You are being evaluated on the total pattern, not one isolated item.

How to approach the clinical interview

Expect follow-up questions about personal history, stress, relationships, anger/conflict, work behavior, substance use and significant life events. Answer candidly and distinguish current facts from past events. If asked about counseling or medical history, respond to the scope of the question and the lawful process you are in; do not conceal requested information, but do not volunteer unrelated private detail simply because you are nervous.

Federal employment-law context

Under the ADA, disability-related inquiries and medical examinations are generally restricted before a conditional job offer. Post-offer examinations may be required if applicants entering the same job category are treated consistently, and medical information is subject to confidentiality requirements. An earlier polygraph, CVSA, interview, or questionnaire does not automatically make medical or disability-related questions permissible. Answer questions authorized for the stage honestly and follow the agency's instructions.

Chapter 8: The Medical Examination

A licensed physician (often chosen or approved by the agency) will confirm you meet the medical standards for the job, which typically include vision, hearing, cardiovascular health, and musculoskeletal function, along with a drug screen.

- Bring a complete list of current medications and past major diagnoses or surgeries — omissions here can resurface as a credibility issue even when the underlying condition wouldn't have disqualified you on its own.
- If you wear corrective lenses, confirm your agency's uncorrected and corrected vision standards in advance, since some agencies have specific uncorrected minimums.
- Follow the agency's instructions regarding medications and substances that could affect testing. Do not stop or alter a prescribed medication without guidance from the prescribing clinician; disclose prescribed medications through the process the medical examiner or collection site provides.
- If you have a chronic condition that's well-controlled (asthma, diabetes, etc.), bring documentation from your treating physician showing it's managed — this is usually more useful than trying to minimize it.

From the Field: Why the medical stage matters

Police work can involve driving, shift work, protective equipment, sudden exertion, firearms, emergency response, and long periods of concentration. The medical evaluation is not asking whether you are a perfect physical specimen. It is assessing job-related ability and safety under the applicable standard. Be accurate about medications and history, bring requested documentation, and never change prescribed treatment merely to influence an exam.

What to Expect at the Medical Stage

A peace-officer medical evaluation is job-related and can include review of medical history plus examination of systems relevant to essential job functions. Specific standards vary. California POST's current medical resources, for example, include detailed vision and hearing guidance and medication-related impairment considerations. Texas uses agency-selected practitioners and state medical/psychological declarations for appointment.

Before the appointment

Follow the agency's instructions about fasting, exercise, caffeine, identification, eyewear/contact lenses, hearing devices, medications, records and forms. Bring an accurate medication list. Do not stop or alter a prescribed medication merely to influence a hiring exam; discuss medication changes with the prescribing clinician and disclose as the examining process requires.

Drug screening

Many agencies require controlled-substance screening, but testing panels, timing, prescription-verification procedures and consequences differ. Follow the collection site's instructions, identify legitimate prescriptions through the designated medical-review process when asked, and do not attempt dilution, substitution or masking.

Vision and hearing

Do not assume a single national uncorrected-vision, corrected-vision, color-vision or hearing threshold. Ask the hiring agency for its current standard. If you use corrective lenses, hearing aids or have prior surgery, bring documentation when requested and allow the examining clinician—not internet forums—to determine whether you meet the job-related standard.

Chapter 9: A Background Investigator's Do's and Don'ts

DO	DON'T
Disclose everything the form asks for, even old or embarrassing items.	Assume something is 'too old' or 'too minor' to mention.
Keep your story consistent across the PHS, interview, polygraph, and psych evaluation.	Give a different version of events depending on who's asking.
Respond to investigator requests quickly and completely.	Go silent, miss deadlines, or make the investigator chase you down.
List a genuinely mixed set of references, including peers and former roommates.	List only close friends and family who are guaranteed to flatter you.
Give references and collateral contacts a heads-up that they may be contacted.	Coach references on exactly what to say.
Gather a current phone number and a current email address for every reference yourself.	Assume the investigator or the online system will track people down for you.
Confirm contact information directly with each person before you submit anything.	Rely on an old number or email you haven't verified in years.
Clean up your financial habits and social media presence going forward.	Scrub or delete accounts right before applying.
Ask your recruiter or investigator directly if you're unsure whether to disclose something.	Guess, minimize, or leave a question blank because you're not sure how it will look.
Disclose a past conflict with an ex-partner or former roommate yourself, with context.	Hope it doesn't come up, or that we won't find the person.
Bring documentation for anything you can (court dispositions, medical records, pay stubs).	Rely only on your memory for dates, amounts, or case numbers.
Treat every stage — even informal-feeling ones — as part of the formal record.	Assume a friendly investigator or casual setting means the stakes are lower.

Chapter 10: PHS Preparation Checklists

Gather these before you start your Personal History Statement — whether it's a paper packet or an online profile through a system like Guardian or eSOPH. Having them on hand prevents the vague, inconsistent answers that create red flags, and gathering accurate contact information is your responsibility, not the investigator's.

Documents to gather

☐	Certified birth certificate and Social Security card
☐	Driver's license and complete driving record (request your official record from the DMV)
☐	High school diploma / transcripts and college transcripts or degrees
☐	Military DD-214 and any service records, if applicable
☐	Marriage certificate(s) and divorce decree(s), if applicable
☐	Last 2–3 years of tax returns or W-2s
☐	Credit report (request your free annual report to review before investigators do)
☐	Certified copies of any court dispositions, including expunged or sealed cases
☐	Complete list of every address for the lookback period, with approximate dates
☐	Complete list of every employer for the lookback period, with supervisor names, current phone numbers, and current email addresses
☐	List of professional, personal, and collateral references who know you well and will speak candidly

Habits to build in the weeks before you apply

☐	Write out your personal timeline (schools, jobs, addresses, roommates) so dates are consistent everywhere
☐	Review your own social media as a stranger would see it
☐	Contact every reference and collateral contact yourself first to confirm a current phone number and a current, regularly checked email address
☐	Tell every reference and collateral contact they may be contacted, so they aren't caught off guard by a call or an automated email from a system like Guardian or eSOPH
☐	Address any outstanding minor legal, financial, or driving issues you can reasonably resolve
☐	Get in the habit of sleeping and eating well in the week leading up to any testing stage

Reference and collateral contact worksheet

Use this to plan a genuinely diverse reference list before you fill out your PHS or online profile. Confirm the phone number and email address directly with each person yourself — don't guess or rely on an old contact saved from years ago. Aim to fill in every row, not just the easy ones.

Relationship type	Name	Phone (confirmed)	Email (confirmed)	Notes
Current or recent supervisor				
Teacher, professor, or coach (official)				
Parent or family member				
Roommate or former roommate				
Landlord or property manager				
Recreational teammate / hobby peer				
Long-term friend outside work/family/school				
Neighbor (informal)				
Former significant other, if applicable				

Chapter 11: Final Thoughts from the Investigator's Desk

After years of doing this work, the pattern I see over and over is simple: candidates who are forthcoming — even about things they're not proud of, and even about the parts of their life that only a roommate or an old friend would know — come through the process in far better shape than candidates who try to manage their image. Investigators aren't looking for flawless people. We're looking for people we can trust to tell the truth when it's inconvenient, because that's exactly what the job will ask of you every day you wear the uniform.

The same goes for the practical, unglamorous parts of the process — gathering accurate contact information, keeping a consistent timeline, double-checking an email address. None of that is the investigator's job to do for you. Treating your own file with that level of care, before you ever submit it, tells us something about how you'll handle responsibility on the job.

If there's one piece of advice worth remembering above all the others in this guide, it's this: whatever is in your past, it is almost always easier to explain than to explain away.

Good luck. The profession needs people willing to be honest about who they are — that's exactly the kind of candidate this process is built to find.

Chapter 12: Command Interview, Final Review, and Conditional Selection

Some agencies use a chief, sheriff, command-staff, hiring-board or final suitability interview after other competitive stages; others make a final review from the completed file. This stage is not universal, but it is common enough that applicants should prepare for it.

From the Recruiter's Desk: The final interview

A final or command interview is not the time to unveil a more polished version of your history. Senior leaders may be looking at the same qualities assessed throughout the process: judgment, accountability, communication, preparation, and whether your reasons for joining align with public service. Know the agency and community, but speak in your own voice. If a difficult fact comes up, use the same truthful account you gave earlier.

What may be evaluated

Expect emphasis on judgment, maturity, motivation, department fit, accountability, communication and any unresolved issue surfaced earlier. Treat the interview as a continuation of the official process. Do not assume a command interview is merely ceremonial because you have already completed a background.

Be ready to explain your application history

Know why you want this agency, what you learned during the process, what you understand about the community and job, and how your past experiences prepared you for public service. If an earlier disclosure is raised, use the same truthful facts you provided before; do not "improve" the story for senior leadership.

Conditional selection and waiting

A conditional offer may still depend on successful completion of background, medical, psychological, drug-screening or other lawful requirements. Continue to follow reporting instructions until your actual appointment date. If something material changes—citation, arrest, job discipline, address, contact information, prescription relevant to an exam, or other item the agency requires—report it through the designated channel.

Chapter 13: Academy Entry, Probation, and Field Training

Getting hired is the beginning of professional evaluation, not the end. Academy standards vary by state, but recruits should expect a combination of academics, report writing, practical skills, physical conditioning, firearms and other defensive skills, law, ethics, scenario performance and professional conduct. After academy graduation, many agencies require a structured field-training or police-training program and a probationary period.

From the Field: Getting hired is not the finish line

I have watched people focus so intensely on receiving an offer that they forget what the offer begins. The academy, field training, and probation will keep evaluating your integrity, learning ability, fitness, report writing, judgment, teamwork, emotional control, and response to correction. Show up teachable. The instructor or field-training officer is not asking whether you already know everything; they are asking whether you can learn, apply feedback, and perform safely.

Start preparing before day one

Arrive with reading/writing habits, baseline fitness, sleep discipline, time-management systems, professional communication and a willingness to be coached. Do not arrive trying to demonstrate tactics you learned online. The academy will teach the approved method and evaluate your ability to learn and safely apply it.

The same qualities keep appearing

Across testing, background, psychological screening, academy and field training, the recurring themes are remarkably consistent: integrity, judgment, communication, learning ability, emotional regulation, reliability, teamwork and willingness to accept correction. The hiring process is not a collection of unrelated hurdles; it is a series of different lenses on many of the same job-related qualities.

Chapter 14: Master Applicant Preparation Plan

Use this as a planning framework and adjust it to the agency's actual timeline.

When	Primary work	Deliverable
60–90 days before applying	Read agency standards; obtain records; build master timeline; begin test-specific fitness and written prep.	Verified eligibility + document folder
30–60 days	Practice exact written test format; build oral-board story bank; resolve contact information; review driving/credit/legal records.	Application-ready data set
0–30 days	Submit carefully; monitor email; continue PAT training; rehearse oral board; update changes immediately.	Clean application + testing readiness
Background phase	Complete PHS from records; answer investigator requests promptly; track corrections; prepare references without coaching.	Complete, consistent background file
Post-offer/final stages	Follow medical/psych/polygraph instructions; maintain professionalism; prepare for command interview and academy start.	Appointment-ready candidate

Questions to Ask the Recruiter Before You Test

What written test is used, and is there an official study guide? What PAT events and standards apply? Are prior written/PAT scores transferable? Is there a PHS or background packet I can review before applying? What documents should I begin gathering? What are the agency's current automatic disqualifiers and case-by-case considerations? Does the agency use a polygraph or other detection-of-deception exam? At what point are medical and psychological evaluations conducted? How long are scores or eligibility-list placements valid? Who should I contact if something changes after I apply?

Applicant "Red Flag" Behaviors That Are Avoidable

Missing deadlines; ignoring recruiter or investigator messages; guessing dates instead of checking records; changing an answer because you think the new version sounds better; coaching references; hiding prior applications; deleting social-media accounts immediately before backgrounds solely to conceal content; failing to report a material change when instructed; arriving late or unprepared for testing; arguing with evaluators about standards; and relying on online rumors instead of the agency's written instructions.

Chapter 15: Glossary of Common Hiring Terms

Conditional offer: An offer that remains dependent on completion of specified pre-employment requirements. PHS/PHQ: Personal History Statement/Questionnaire used to collect detailed background information. PAT/PFT/POPAT: Agency-specific physical ability/fitness testing acronyms. POST: A state Peace Officer Standards and Training body; exact name and authority vary by state. NTN/FrontLine: A national testing provider and one law-enforcement testing system used by participating agencies. Collateral reference: A person identified during the investigation who was not necessarily selected by the applicant. Detection of deception: Umbrella term that may include polygraph or other technologies where lawful and agency-approved. Suitability: A job-related determination that an applicant meets the agency's standards; it is not necessarily the same as merely meeting minimum legal eligibility.

Appendix A: Sources & Further Reading

The following official or primary-source resources were reviewed for factual verification in this expanded 2026 edition. References are provided so readers can confirm current requirements directly. The presence of a source here does not imply sponsorship or endorsement, and this guide does not reproduce proprietary test content, vendor interfaces, logos, or protected third-party forms. Always prioritize the hiring agency's own announcement and instructions.

- California POST - Peace Officer Candidate Selection Standards
- California POST - Peace Officer Candidate Selection Process
- California POST - PELLETB Applicant FAQs
- California POST - Interviewing Peace Officer Candidates
- California POST - Background Investigation Manual
- California POST - Psychological Screening Manual
- California POST - Medical Screening Manual
- National Testing Network - FrontLine National Law Enforcement Testing
- Texas Commission on Law Enforcement - Model Policy Guidance / Hiring Procedures
- Texas Commission on Law Enforcement - Forms and Applications
- Washington State Criminal Justice Training Commission - Employment / agency hiring examples
- U.S. EEOC - Employment Tests and Selection Procedures
- U.S. EEOC - Pre-Employment Inquiries and Medical Questions & Examinations
- Consumer Financial Protection Bureau - Employment Background and Credit Report Applicant Rights
- California POST - December 2025 Background Investigation Manual Revision Summary
- ADA.gov - The ADA and Hiring Police Officers
- U.S. Department of Labor - Employee Polygraph Protection Act Fact Sheet #36
- Florida Department of Law Enforcement - CJSTC Forms (background/certification examples)

• Boston Police Department - History (watch established 1631; department established 1854)

• U.S. Bureau of Justice Statistics - Contacts Between Police and the Public, 2022 (published October 2024)

• Gallup - Confidence in Institutions historical trends (police confidence series, updated 2026)

This guide offers general information based on common practices across U.S. law enforcement agencies. Specific requirements, disqualifiers, procedures, and background-investigation platforms vary by state and department — always rely on your own agency's official instructions.

Research currency: Expanded edition researched and verified through September 1, 2026. Laws, state standards, vendor test formats, and agency policies can change after publication. Verify current requirements directly with the hiring agency and relevant state licensing/POST authority.

Author experience note: Professional observations are based on the anonymous experience described in the opening disclosure. They are not presented as findings from controlled research. Research notes identify outside authorities used for factual or legal context.

Publication Integrity Note

This edition was reviewed for third-party source use before publication. Factual statements drawn from public materials were paraphrased or summarized; short official names and competency labels are retained only where needed for accurate identification. No proprietary examination questions, answer keys, copyrighted vendor screenshots, third-party logos, or proprietary background-platform forms are intentionally reproduced. If a future edition adds outside photographs, graphics, excerpts, or sample forms, permission and licensing should be reviewed before publication.

PASSING THE BACKGROUND

PEACE OFFICER APPLICANT TOOLKIT

Original worksheets, self-audits, trackers, and stage-by-stage preparation tools for use with Passing the Background

Developed from 30 years of sworn service and 15 years conducting background investigations

Important: This toolkit is for organization and honest preparation. It is not an agency Personal History Statement, does not replace official forms, and should never be used to conceal, minimize, rehearse around, or manipulate information requested by a hiring agency.

Toolkit Contents

Click a tool name to jump directly to it.

Use this toolkit correctly: Complete it from records and your best good-faith recollection. When an official form asks a question, answer the official question exactly as instructed. If your worksheet conflicts with an official record or later recollection, correct the official submission through the agency's permitted process rather than trying to force consistency.

Tool 1: Master Applicant Timeline

Build one chronological reference before completing applications, a PHS, interviews, or supplemental forms.

← Back to Toolkit Contents

Date range	City / address	School / employer / activity	Supervisor / roommate / contact	Major event / note

Investigator perspective: A timeline is a memory aid, not a script. Approximate dates should be identified as approximate when the agency permits; never invent precision you do not actually know.

Tool 2: Agency Research Worksheet

Prepare for the specific agency rather than for a generic police hiring process.

← Back to Toolkit Contents

Research item	Your notes
Agency mission / values	
Jurisdiction & communities served	
Chief / sheriff and command structure	
Patrol / specialty assignments	
Recent initiatives or strategic priorities	
Hiring stages and order	
Written test used	
PAT format / standards	
Background/PHS platform or form	

Research item	Your notes
Agency-specific disqualifier guidance	
Why this agency fits your goals	
Questions to ask recruiter	

Tool 3: Employment History Master Worksheet

Create a complete employer history before you enter information into an agency system.

← Back to Toolkit Contents

Employer	Dates	Position	Supervisor	Phone / email	Reason left

For each employer, record any discipline, attendance issues, performance plans, resignations in lieu of discipline, termination, workplace investigations, or other matters if the agency's questions require them. Use a separate page if needed.

Employer	Issue / event	Approx. date	Outcome	Records or contact who can verify

Employer	Issue / event	Approx. date	Outcome	Records or contact who can verify

Tool 4: Residence & Roommate History Worksheet

Reconstruct your lifetime residence and roommate history as a private master record, then use the period required by each agency's form. Include landlord/property-manager and roommate contact information.

← Back to Toolkit Contents

Address / city	From	To	Roommate / co-tenant	Phone / email	Landlord / manager

Do not curate the list: If an official PHS asks for all roommates or cohabitants, list them according to the form's instructions - not only the people you believe will give favorable references.

Tool 5: Education, Military & Volunteer History

Organize institutions and service that may be verified during the process.

← Back to Toolkit Contents

Organization / school	Dates	Role / program	Contact	Credential / outcome	Issue to disclose?

☐ Transcripts or completion records located

☐ Military discharge/service records located, if applicable

☐ Volunteer coordinator contact confirmed

☐ Dates cross-checked against master timeline

Tool 6: Prior Law-Enforcement Application Log

Track every prior application so you can accurately answer questions about previous hiring processes.

← Back to Toolkit Contents

Agency	Position	Applied	Stage reached	Outcome / withdrew	Background / polygraph / psych?	Contact / notes

Agency	Position	Applied	Stage reached	Outcome / withdrew	Background / polygraph / psych?	Contact / notes

Why this matters: Prior applications can create records that later agencies may request or compare. Record the outcome accurately; do not guess why an agency made a decision if you were not told.

Tool 7: Legal, Driving & Financial History Organizer

Gather facts and records before you answer official questions.

← Back to Toolkit Contents

Legal / court matters

Date	Jurisdiction	Incident / case	Disposition / outcome	Documents obtained

Driving history

Date	Citation / collision / suspension	Jurisdiction	Outcome	Record obtained

Date	Citation / collision / suspension	Jurisdiction	Outcome	Record obtained

Financial matters

Account / issue	Approx. date	Status	Resolution / payment plan	Documentation

Tool 8: Reference & Collateral Contact Tracker

Confirm accurate contact information and build a diverse, truthful reference list.

← Back to Toolkit Contents

Name	Relationship	Years known	Phone confirmed	Email confirmed	Last confirmed	Notes

Name	Relationship	Years known	Phone confirmed	Email confirmed	Last confirmed	Notes

☐ Current/recent supervisor

☐ Long-term friend

☐ Roommate/former roommate

☐ Neighbor

☐ Landlord/property manager

☐ Teacher/coach/mentor if requested

☐ Other relationship specifically required by the PHS

No coaching: A heads-up that an investigator may contact someone is appropriate. Telling a reference what to say, what not to mention, or how to answer is not.

Tool 9: Disclosure Preparation Worksheet

Organize facts so you can make a complete, straightforward disclosure when the agency asks about an issue.

← Back to Toolkit Contents

Disclosure 1

Prompt	Your factual notes
What happened?	
When did it happen and how often?	
What was your role / responsibility?	
What was the outcome?	
What changed afterward?	
What record or person can verify the facts?	
Where have you already disclosed this (application/PHS/etc.)?	

Disclosure 2

Prompt	Your factual notes
What happened?	
When did it happen and how often?	
What was your role / responsibility?	
What was the outcome?	
What changed afterward?	
What record or person can verify the facts?	
Where have you already disclosed this (application/PHS/etc.)?	

Disclosure 3

Prompt	Your factual notes
What happened?	
When did it happen and how often?	
What was your role / responsibility?	
What was the outcome?	
What changed afterward?	
What record or person can verify the facts?	
Where have you already disclosed this (application/PHS/etc.)?	

Purpose: This framework is for completeness, not persuasion. Do not omit aggravating facts, invent mitigating facts, or rehearse a version designed to defeat a polygraph, psychological evaluation, or investigator interview.

Tool 10: PHS Self-Audit & Consistency Check

Audit your official submission for completeness and internal consistency before you submit, when the agency permits review.

← Back to Toolkit Contents

☐ Every required question has an answer or the agency-approved equivalent of N/A.

☐ Names, aliases, addresses, dates, employers, schools, and phone/email information have been checked.

☐ Employment gaps are accounted for.

☐ Residence dates align reasonably with school/employment dates.

☐ All prior law-enforcement applications requested by the form are listed.

☐ Legal and driving matters requested by the form are listed.

☐ Financial matters requested by the form are answered completely.

☐ Military history is complete, if applicable.

☐ Reference contact information was confirmed directly.

☐ Disclosures are consistent with records in your possession.

☐ Any estimated dates are handled according to agency instructions rather than presented as invented exact dates.

☐ You saved a permitted copy or notes of what you submitted for later reference.

☐ You know the agency's process for correcting an error discovered after submission.

Correction / discrepancy log

Date found	Section / question	What needs correction	Correct information	Agency notified / method	Resolved

Tool 11: Oral Board STAR Story Builder

Prepare real examples without memorizing scripted answers.

← Back to Toolkit Contents

Story 1

Element	Notes
Situation - enough context to understand the event	
Task - your responsibility	
Action - what you personally did	
Result - what happened	
Reflection - what you learned / would repeat or change	
Competencies this story may demonstrate	

Story 2

Element	Notes
Situation - enough context to understand the event	
Task - your responsibility	
Action - what you personally did	
Result - what happened	
Reflection - what you learned / would repeat or change	
Competencies this story may demonstrate	

Story 3

Element	Notes
Situation - enough context to understand the event	
Task - your responsibility	
Action - what you personally did	
Result - what happened	
Reflection - what you learned / would repeat or change	
Competencies this story may demonstrate	

Element	Notes
Current POST example: California POST currently requires oral interviews to assess six factors: experience, problem-solving, communication skills, interest/motivation, interpersonal skills, and community involvement/awareness. Other jurisdictions may use different competencies; follow the agency's process.	

Tool 12: Investigator Request & Document Tracker

Respond promptly and keep a record of what was requested, supplied, and still outstanding.

← Back to Toolkit Contents

Date requested	Requested item	Due	Sent / completed	Method	Follow-up / status

☐ Court dispositions

☐ Driving record

☐ Employment verification information

☐ Transcripts / education records

☐ Military records, if applicable

☐ Financial documentation requested by investigator

☐ Clarification or supplemental statement requested by investigator

Tool 13: 48 Hours Before Each Stage Checklists

Use these as final readiness checks. Agency instructions always control.

← Back to Toolkit Contents

Written examination

☐ Confirm time, location, parking, identification, and permitted materials.

☐ Review the specific test provider's official candidate guide.

☐ Sleep normally; avoid last-minute cramming.

☐ Plan to arrive early.

Physical ability test

☐ Confirm exact events, standards, clothing, and equipment rules.

☐ Hydrate and eat normally; do not experiment with new supplements or routines.

☐ Prepare required identification/forms.

☐ Follow agency medical/participation instructions.

Oral board

☐ Review agency research and job announcement.

☐ Review real STAR examples; do not memorize canned answers.

☐ Confirm professional attire, route, arrival time, and required documents.

☐ Prepare concise questions if the panel permits them.

Background interview / PHS

☐ Review the copy/notes of what you submitted if permitted.

☐ Bring requested records and your discrepancy/correction log.

☐ Write down any newly remembered item that may need clarification.

☐ Do not alter your story to make it sound better; correct errors directly.

Polygraph / detection-of-deception exam

- ☐ Follow the examiner's instructions.
- ☐ Review prior disclosures for accuracy, not for rehearsed wording.
- ☐ Sleep and eat normally.
- ☐ Do not use countermeasures or attempt to manipulate the examination.

Psychological evaluation

- ☐ Follow scheduling and paperwork instructions.
- ☐ Bring only records requested by the evaluator/agency.
- ☐ Sleep normally and answer assessment/interview questions candidly.
- ☐ Do not try to reverse-engineer a desirable personality profile.

Medical / drug screening

- ☐ Follow clinic and agency instructions exactly.
- ☐ Bring identification and requested medication/medical information.
- ☐ Do not stop or alter prescribed medication merely to affect screening; discuss medication changes with the prescribing clinician.
- ☐ Ask the clinic how prescribed medications should be documented if instructions are unclear.

Tool 14: Post-Interview / Final Review Log

Capture factual follow-up items after a stage without rewriting history.

← Back to Toolkit Contents

Date / stage	Question or issue to follow up	Document / correction needed	Who to contact	Completed	Notes

Date / stage	Question or issue to follow up	Document / correction needed	Who to contact	Completed	Notes

Final file readiness

- ☐ All investigator requests answered by the stated deadline.
- ☐ Any discovered error was corrected using the agency's process.
- ☐ Contact information remains current.
- ☐ You can be reached by phone and email.
- ☐ You have not coached references or attempted to influence collateral contacts.
- ☐ You continue to follow the hiring agency's instructions rather than generic advice.

Final reminder: A strong applicant file is organized, responsive, complete, and candid. These tools are designed to reduce preventable errors - not to make an applicant appear to have a different history.

Tool 15: Pre-Polygraph / CVSA Questionnaire Self-Review

Use this worksheet after reading the agency's actual instructions. It is an accuracy and disclosure check - not a prediction sheet for test questions.

Self-review prompt	Your notes / action needed
Did I answer every questionnaire item exactly as instructed?	
Did any question remind me of information missing from my PHS/application?	
Are any dates, frequencies, amounts, or circumstances uncertain?	
Is there an answer I need the examiner to clarify before I can answer accurately?	

Self-review prompt	Your notes / action needed
Do I need to correct an earlier submission through the agency process?	
What supporting record, if requested, could clarify a factual issue?	
Have I avoided rehearsing or changing truthful answers merely because I fear a reaction?	

REMEMBER
The questionnaire can indicate subject areas that may be discussed, but it should not be used to reverse-engineer the examination. Review it for completeness and candor. Your objective is 100% honesty, not a manufactured response.

Source Notes & Further Reading

These tools are original applicant-preparation worksheets. External authorities informed limited process descriptions and are credited here.

California Commission on Peace Officer Standards and Training (POST). Peace Officer Candidate Selection Standards and Candidate Selection Process. Current POST materials describe the application, reading/writing assessment, physical ability testing where used, oral interview, background investigation, medical evaluation, and psychological evaluation, while noting that local agencies may impose additional standards.

California POST. Background Investigation Manual: Guidelines for the Investigator, revised December 2025. Used to verify the current role of the PHS and the requirement that background dimensions be considered in California peace-officer investigations.

California POST. Personal History Statement - Peace Officer (POST 2-251, 1/2024). Used only as a reference for the types of historical information applicants may be required to assemble. This toolkit does not reproduce or replace the POST form.

California POST. Oral Interview requirements. Used to verify the six California POST interview factors referenced in Tool 11.

Selective Service System. Who Needs to Register. Used to verify the current federal registration ages, covered populations, and limited exceptions discussed in Chapter 4.

U.S. National Archives and Records Administration. Military Service Records and What Is an Official Military Personnel File (OMPF)? Used to verify OMPF contents and the eVetRecs/SF-180 request options discussed in Chapter 4.

Official source links should be accessed through the agency or POST website because forms, regulations, manuals, and URLs can change.

Jurisdiction warning: California POST is used as a detailed public example, not as a nationwide rulebook. Peace-officer selection requirements differ by state, agency, collective-bargaining/civil-service framework, and local policy.

Additional research supporting Chapter 6

U.S. Department of Labor. Fact Sheet #36: Employee Polygraph Protection Act of 1988. Used for the federal definition of polygraph/lie-detector devices and government-employer exclusion from EPPA.

National Research Council. The Polygraph and Lie Detection. National Academies Press, 2003. Used for the discussion of scientific limitations and the distinction between specific-incident and screening applications.

National Institute of Justice / Office of Justice Programs. Assessing the Validity of Voice Stress Analysis Tools in a Jail Setting, 2007. Used for the independent evaluation of CVSA/voice-stress performance in that study.

Hollien, H., Harnsberger, J.D., Martin, C.A., and Hollien, K.A. Evaluation of the NITV CVSA. Journal of Forensic Sciences 53(1), 2008. Used for an additional independent CVSA evaluation summarized in Chapter 6.

www.ingramcontent.com/pod-product-compliance
Lightning Source LLC
LaVergne TN
LVHW010738061126
851857LV00014B/1532